THE ELEMENTS OF SPEECHWRITING AND PUBLIC SPEAKING

OTHER PAPERBACK TITLES OF INTEREST

The Elements of Style
William Strunk, Jr., and E. B. White

The Elements of Grammar
Margaret D. Shertzer

The Elements of Editing
Arthur Plotnik

Writing That Means Business
Ellen Roddick

The Art of Readable Writing
Rudolf Flesch

The

ELEMENTS OF
SPEECHWRITING
AND
PUBLIC SPEAKING

Jeff Scott Cook

COLLIER BOOKS
MACMILLAN PUBLISHING COMPANY
New York

COLLIER MACMILLAN CANADA
Toronto

MAXWELL MACMILLAN INTERNATIONAL
New York Oxford Singapore Sydney

Collier Books
Macmillan Publishing Company
866 Third Avenue
New York, NY 10022

Collier Macmillan Canada, Inc.
1200 Eglinton Avenue East, Suite 200
Don Mills, Ontario M3C 3N1

Library of Congress Cataloging-in-Publication Data
Cook, Jeff Scott.
    The elements of speechwriting and public speaking / Jeff Scott
Cook.—1st Collier Books ed.
        p. cm.
    Includes bibliographical references and index.
    ISBN 0-02-042782-4
    1. Speechwriting. 2. Public speaking. 3. English language—
Rhetoric. I. Title.
    PN4142.C66   1991   90-27038   CIP
    808.5—dc20

Macmillan books are available at special discounts for bulk pur-
chases for sales promotions, premiums, fund-raising, or educational
use. For details, contact:

    Special Sales Director
    Macmillan Publishing Company
    866 Third Avenue
    New York, NY 10022

First Collier Books Edition 1991

10 9 8 7 6 5 4

Printed in the United States of America

For Jan and Cameron

CONTENTS

PREFACE

The ability to speak confidently and well is a talent universally admired and envied. But it is more than just a novelty, like juggling. The ability to hold an audience—to be heard by those who matter—is a crucial skill at any age.

When we are born, survival itself depends on gaining the interest and understanding of parents. As we grow, we learn that words, not wails, are the preferred medium of communication with people in authority. In school, our sense of belonging and our very identity depends on the willing attention and acceptance of teachers and schoolmates. Our odds of getting both are vastly improved if we can speak comfortably and, as the choir director would say, with feeling.

On the job we are rewarded for speaking well at sales presentations, staff meetings, and customer and employee gatherings of all kinds. Through our many social affiliations, we learn that life is richer for those who can confidently "say a few words." It's great fun to get a few laughs at the annual banquet, gratifying to make convincing proposals to the community council, and wonderful to successfully ask for a raise in pay.

Then, on an otherwise normal day, something touches, angers, or wounds us so deeply that we must stand and speak out. Whether anybody agrees, it doesn't matter. At that moment, being able to give a good speech is more than a convenience, more than one of many ways to get a bigger paycheck, a greener park on Elm Street, or a louder round of applause at the party. At that moment, in gathering the courage to speak and the skill to do it well, we flex the mightiest muscle of civilization. Speaking up on what matters can be the proudest (and possibly the most important) moment of one's life.

No one says speech making is easy. Some people spend hours preparing even the most informal speech. While I believe people fret far too much about it, I'll be the first to acknowledge that speech making can be difficult—even agonizing.

For beginners as well as for many practiced voices, the challenge of speech making is the same: to quiet fears of the unknown, resist the call of procrastination, quicken a sluggish brain, and, not least, keep believing that you must have something worthwhile to say or they wouldn't have invited you. But despite our best intentions, as the days preceding the speech dwindle to hours and minutes, we tend to smother ourselves with self-criticism and doubt. Will I make some horrible gaffe? What if I get there late? What if I forget my notes? What if the venue has been changed to another building? What if the date has been changed to another night? To last night? And look at these clothes. I should have dressed up more. Will my voice be loud enough? I've never checked that. It probably won't, but I doubt anyone will let me know. If only I had even a shimmer of the grace of Kennedy, the humor of Will Rogers, the authority of Cronkite. But no, I can't change who I am. I'll just have to get up there and be myself. But that's the problem, isn't it?

How does anyone survive this? How can we get past this

psychological torment to experience the exhilaration, pride, and deep feeling of self-worth that accompanies confident self-expression?

The answer will not surprise you: by study and practice. The truth is that simple, but remarkably hard for some to accept. Only a fool would expect a person who'd never touched a violin to be able to pick it up and play like Heifetz or Perlman. Yet many people expect themselves to be able to speak as well as, say, Winston Churchill—if not on the first time out, then certainly on the second or third!

What self-destructive folly. Learning to do any complex task well takes time and effort. But fortunately, it's remarkable how even a passing awareness of the fundamentals of public speaking can cut the fog of anxiety and confusion that surrounds it. Everyone knows or has heard of a timid soul who, after learning a few things about speaking, became salesperson of the month, head auctioneer, chair of the United Fund, political powerhouse, or some such citizen of visible accomplishment.

Those who can speak well in public are not all geniuses, charismatics, or extroverted children of the stage. With a little study and practice, anyone—and that means *you*—can write an effective speech and deliver it with power and grace. You know you can. You've seen people do it and you know they are no better than you. So take my advice, study it.

If you're not now a fair or good public speaker, reading this book and combining it with practice and observation is a good way to become one. The book covers the basics of speech preparation and delivery, and more. If you apply the principles and use the techniques within these pages, I guarantee that the applause will be louder and stronger. I guarantee you'll be more successful at any job that requires clear communication of thoughts and feelings. And I guarantee you'll come to fear it less and enjoy it more. But please don't stop with this book. People have been writing furiously about speech making for generations. It's a rich, rich collection of enjoyable and instructive writing. A good selection of it is available in most libraries.

For you, the beginner, I hope this book calms your nerves and steels your spirit. I know it will give you a great deal of useful knowledge. For you, the practiced speaker, the book should serve as a reassuring and lively compendium of lessons learned the hard way.

If you want a worthwhile challenge, you'll find one in public speaking. If it's conviviality you seek, you'll find that, too. Whatever your reasons or goals, in speaking your mind, your mind will grow. And you'll experience your world at a deeper, more stimulating level than you ever thought possible.

Part One

PREPARATION

1

KNOW YOUR
AUDIENCE AND
SETTING

A SPEECH GONE BAD

The first secret of good speaking is knowing who's listening. I learned this lesson the hard way some years back when I worked as a speechwriter for a large bank. I reported to an outgoing man in his mid-forties whom I shall call "Rudy."

One day Rudy was invited to speak to a group of public school administrators in Vancouver, Washington, a happy little burg about 150 miles from our offices in Seattle. The letter of invitation said they wanted him to speak on "community relations," with an eye on business relations with the schools. In other words, they left it open.

Rudy was delighted with the invitation. He was itching to give a serious speech and I was tired of writing fluff. So off we went. Selecting the main points was easy. Rudy was bubbling with hot opinions on education and business. Soon we had a punchy speech on paper. It began by hammering away on a "survival of the fittest" theme, with the clear implication that the public schools were foundering because they'd lost the competitive edge. The speech then progressed to argue how our schools *might* survive if administrators would take a more "businesslike" approach to their work; stress return on investment, quality control, service to the customer, and all that.

Now, Rudy's invitation had been engineered by a former bank employee active in the group. That much we knew because the man's name was on the letter of invitation. What we *didn't* know, among other things, was that he had assured his fellow members that Rudy was a *nice guy,* a *supporter* of the public schools, and a highly *entertaining* and *inspirational* speaker!

Embarrassing as it is to admit, the only serious research we did into the event or audience was to confirm the where and when. Everything else was irrelevant. Or so it seemed.

When the fateful day arrived, Rudy and I boarded a plane and soon entered the local restaurant meeting hall.

The event turned out to be the group's anniversary meeting. And it was not, as we had assumed, a gathering of school administrators only. Instead, it was a *joint* gathering of education *and* business leaders, a group dedicated to building trust between private business and public schools. In the vernacular of the 1960s, it was a love-in. And the agenda bore it out—long and bloated with committee reports detailing all the wonderful ways in which the Vancouver public schools were improving their services to the citizenry by working closely with the business community! Against this melody of mutual admiration, Rudy's message would clash, hitting not a keynote but a sour note.

The audience numbered about seventy. Like Rudy, most were men. Unlike Rudy, most were Democrats. They dressed well, but casually, in the uniform of the day: tweed sport coats, gray wool slacks, loafers. As for the room, it was stifling. Afternoon summer sun slammed through the bare, floor-to-ceiling windows. There was no discernable ventilation.

Rudy was ninth on the agenda. Ninth. In the two hours between the opening gavel and his warm introduction, no fewer than twelve people mounted the podium to describe yet another way in which their schools had become more "businesslike." Astoundingly, no breaks had been scheduled. After forty minutes, people were seriously uncomfortable. After an hour and a half, they were ready to kill. Wool pants stuck to seats. Limbs ached. Bladders seared. Brains screamed for mercy. But there was no mercy, for Rudy was next.

During the eternity Rudy had waited, he realized his speech was a bomb. Still, he was a man of conviction. More importantly, he was a man with little talent for improvisation.

When Rudy took his place in front of those seventy surly lumps of sweat-drenched humanity, his $600 pin-striped suit was as crisp as a West Point parade. I wanted to grab him and run, but didn't. He delivered exactly what we'd written.

As I remember it now, the speech had effects similar to nerve gas. Bodies became rigid. Jaws clenched. Eyes grew dark and lifeless. For the twenty minutes Rudy held forth, not a sound came from the crowd, save an occasional gasp.

Then it was over. Five seconds of silence broken by a smattering of weak applause. The emcee rose hurriedly to officially open the bar. But our misery was not over. Dinner had been prepared for all in attendance at the home of an important local citizen. We had to attend because, you see, Rudy had been advertised as the honored guest.

That night on the way home, Rudy and I could only giggle hysterically and moan.

In retrospect, we realized that much of the unpleasantness could have been avoided had we thought longer about

the audience when we were planning the speech. The depth
of our humiliation confirmed once more that of the many
elements of speech making, audience and setting analysis
are among the most important.

What to Learn About Your Audience

You don't need to be on intimate terms with your listeners
to give a good speech. But you do need to know some key
facts about their beliefs and values. In addition, you should
get a feel for speech-making customs of the organization
sponsoring your appearance (if any). And finally, you will
benefit immensely if you are sensitive to the biological state
of your listeners and to the speech environment itself.

LISTENER BIOLOGY AND
THE SPEECH ENVIRONMENT

Contrary to conventional mythology, the most common
enemies of the platform speaker are not hecklers hurling
insults, but waiters dropping trays. Not closed minds blocking ideas, but closed ventilation systems blocking airflow.
Not hard stares numbing the speaker's spirit, but hard
chairs numbing the listeners' butts. Not excess "uhs" in the
speaker's diction, but excess alcohol in the listeners' brains.

It astounds me that speech teachers pay so little attention
to these facts, so obvious from our own experiences as
listeners.

"Nobody ever listened t' reason on an empty stomach,"
said writer Kin Hubbard. An exaggeration? Perhaps. But
the insight reminds us that the body is both gateway and
gatekeeper to the mind.

Moreover, you'll be far ahead of the pack if you think of
your audience as more than everything from the skin in.

Your listeners are people, not objects. To reach them, you must compete with their environment—from the contents of the room around them to the contents of the morning paper to the contents of their stomachs. Be especially mindful of any conditions that prevent your words from being heard. I've made a short list of the *most common* biological and environmental blocks to a successful listening experience:

Biological

> Hearing impairments
> Fatigue
> Hunger
> Mind-altering drugs and alcohol
> Hormones (teenagers)

Environmental

> Noise (telephones, glassware, jackhammers)
> Heat
> Glare from sunlight behind the speaker
> Lack of ventilation
> Uncomfortable seating
> Malfunctioning microphones

This list is not comprehensive, but verified.

Improve Your Chances of Being Heard

There's not much you can do about hormone levels. But many problems are well within your power to avoid. Even if you can't completely solve or prevent them, you'll gain the heartfelt appreciation of your audience by trying.

· Shut the curtains behind you to reduce glare.
· Open some windows or doors to get the air moving.

- Ask the program chair to keep the caterers from clearing tables until you're done speaking.
- Check the microphone early and have it fixed before it's too late.
- Refuse the invitation if the audience won't have had a break in the forty minutes preceding your talk. If that's impractical, give up five minutes of your time to let the audience stretch.
- If you plan to use overhead transparencies or slides, make certain beforehand that the room can be adequately darkened.
- When speaking to elderly people, speak louder. Use clearer diction.
- When speaking to teenagers, speed up.
- Don't talk more than fifteen minutes to an after-dinner audience; ten minutes if alcohol is served.
- Try to avoid speaking just prior to lunch or dinner—people are too hungry to listen.

Dealing with the Program Chair

You are hereby forewarned: Beware of incompetent event organizers. These people frequently go by the title Program Chairperson. My experience with program chairs is that most of them are concerned with only one thing: getting speaker and audience in the same place at the same time. They are not above lying, wheedling, and flattering to achieve their ends.

To attract an audience, they will often exaggerate any or all of the following: the speaker's resumé and abilities, the comfort of the accommodations, and the palatability of the menu. If they don't think a crowd will turn out for just one speaker, they'll try to get three . . . four . . . or however many they think it will take. But in fairness, sometimes the driving force behind agenda bloat is the inability of the program chair to say no. The classic example occurs every national holiday when politicians line up, scripts in hand, like so many tourists at the Blarney Stone.

To entice the speaker, program chairs habitually overestimate the size and clout of the audience. This will be deflating if you're promised a cheering throng of one hundred VIPs in a plush auditorium, but delivered a dozen dour souls in a basement broom closet. It's bad enough when speakers are mistreated. But when *audiences* are abused, look out. Ultimately, the person at the podium is remembered for what goes wrong.

So when you're asked to give a speech, first find out who's in charge of the event. Quiz this person at length about the accommodations and agenda. Then, if you think the situation can be salvaged, make this person do his or her job—which is to give you and your audience the best speaking and listening environment possible. Remember: They need you *at least* as much as you need them.

Questions to Ask About Your Speech Setting

Before you accept the invitation or set pen to paper, you should know the answers to questions like the ones below. Some of the answers may prompt you to reject the invitation, or insist on changes in the agenda or accommodations. At the very least, and without a doubt, knowing answers will build your confidence in what you decide to say.

1. Name and purpose of sponsoring organization?
2. Who is the Program Chair? Her or his telephone number?
3. Date of speech?

4. Time of day of speech?
5. Description of speech location:

   Where is it, *exactly?*
   Size and seating configuration?
   Podium? Table-top lectern? Some place for my notes?
   Can the room be darkened for slides or overheads?
   What is behind the speaker's position? Windows? Exit or entry doors?
   Will I sit in the crowd before my speech or at a head table?
   Is a microphone necessary? Available? Is it a lapel model or a podium-mounted unit? How is the volume controlled? Can you turn it *off* from the podium?

6. How many people will be in the audience? Be realistic.
7. Will food and drinks be served? During or before my speech?
8. What, *exactly,* is the agenda for this event?

   How long am I expected to speak? Is this reasonable for the subject, event, audience?
   What will have happened before I speak? What happens after I speak?
   Who are the other speakers, if any? What is the order of their appearance? What will they be talking about?
   Who will introduce me? Does this person know me? Do I need to help them prepare my introduction?

9. Will I be expected to answer questions after my speech? For how long? Who will moderate this question-answer session?

    10. Will there be TV cameras? Reporters asking ques-
        tions?
    11. Will water be available to me as I speak?

The Ideal Speech Situation

It's worth reminding ourselves at this point that it is possible to pull off a good speech under the most dreadful
of circumstances. When Vice President Hubert Humphrey
ran for the presidency in 1968, a campaign stop was
scheduled at an airstrip in Harlingen, Texas. A crowd of
five thousand waited inside an airplane hangar for four
hours before two commercial jets—one carrying the vice
president and his party and the other carrying the national
press corps—touched down and rolled up to the hangar
doors. The planes swung their noses around and dis-
gorged the candidate and entourage. As this happened, jet
exhaust swept through the steel hangar which, under
the noonday Texas summer sun, was already hotter than
the hubs of hell. For reasons known only to the pilots, the
jet's engines were not turned off as Humphrey spoke.
Nevertheless, the heat, the dust, and the fatigue of the
long wait were no match for Humphrey's ebullient personality. The crowd loved it. Humphrey's unabashed opti-
mism and joy filled the steel cavern with a comforting
melody of hope—the perfect gift for the predominantly
poor community that took the day off when Hubert came
to town.

    Many speaking obstacles can be overcome by sheer zest.
But unless you're handed a dreadful situation, you're better
off working to create an environment conducive to communication. Let's try to describe a good speaking environment
for an informative or persuasive speech to a group of, say,
twenty-five to forty-five people.

Time of day:
10 AM—people are alert, and will not feel hungry until your speech is over.

Day of week:
Thursday or Friday—people have accomplished enough of their weekly regime to be receptive to new ideas.

Place:
Indoors. Maximum seating: fifty. Acoustically friendly—carpeted, ten- to fifteen-foot ceilings, walls with sound-absorbent wallpaper. Soft colors prevail. Exit and entry doors at far end of room from speaker. *Speaker's choice* of podium, lectern, table, stool, or chair positioned front, center. No one else is seated or standing near speaker. Lapel microphone provided with volume control. Plain blue backdrop behind speaker. (Flags to right and left if political event.) Steady, glare-free lighting, controllable by a dimmer knob located inside the room. Temperature: sixty-eight to seventy degrees Fahrenheit. Chairs: movable, straight-backed with cloth-covered cushions. Drinking water is provided next to exit/entrance and near the speaker's position.

Agenda:
Emcee welcomes group, announces the full sequence of events, then introduces you, with no more than 1½ minutes of material that establishes your credentials and humanity. After your 15- to 25-minute presentation, a 5- to 10-minute question-and-answer period is moderated by the emcee. At the end, emcee thanks speaker and audience. The group then breaks for mid-morning refreshments.

Final Notes on Listener Environment

1. You may have noticed that nothing yet has been said about dealing with audiences of different *sizes.* Don't worry. We'll cover this thoroughly in later sections on *delivery.*

2. Different speech *purposes* require different settings. Not every speech is best given under the circumstances just listed. The speech to entertain, for example, is best scheduled for later in the day and in a room too small for the turnout. We'll see more on this as the book progresses.

3. I'm not suggesting for a minute that you'll be able to control every aspect of your speaking environment. But experience teaches that you can control more than you think—especially if you know what you want.

4. Don't exhaust yourself fighting for a walnut podium when a music stand will do. Raw determination and cool thinking will empower you to transcend nearly any annoyance an inexperienced program chairperson might concoct. You'll be surprised at your ability to overcome the unexpected, as this true story illustrates.

For at least ten years now, an early summer conference has been held in Seattle called Women + Business. This three-day affair offers hundreds of speeches and workshops to the public for a single fee. Attendees are given a complete program guide which lists titles and brief descriptions of every speech and workshop, as well as times and room numbers. In 1986, a workshop was scheduled as follows:

Paths to Power—A Colorful Tour Two-Session Workshop. Look at issues and develop strategies for succeeding in today's organization when the issue is not limited to "being a woman"—but a "woman of color." Particular attention will be given to the impact of both corporate and cultural expectations.

The leaders used "women of color" as a euphemism covering a broad range of minority-race females. Who did they expect to show up? Upwardly aspiring black, Asian, and Indian women, and people responsible for enforcing antidiscrimination laws—this would be the natural audience.

But as the starting time for the workshop neared, the two women in charge noticed something very unusual about the unexpectedly large numbers of women filing into the room—most were white. Well, the leaders thought, this is odd, but the show must go on. So they welcomed the group, saying how pleased they were that so many nonminority women were interested in the challenges confronting women of color. A confused look spread across the faces of the audience. After a few minutes, someone in the back asked, "When are we going to get our colors done?"

That comment said it all. A popular variety of workshop at women's gatherings that year offered "personal color consultations," a chance to "do your colors." Women would attend these to learn which fabric colors were most complementary to their skin tone and hair color. And this is what these women thought issues for "women of color" would be about.

This comically ironic misunderstanding brought two wildly different classes of women together. To the great credit of all, after the laughter died down most people stayed put. The leaders huddled and reorganized their presentation. Their determination to communicate made their workshop an unlikely success.

LISTENER PSYCHOLOGY

Because the purpose of speech making is communication, not pontification, the novice who wants to improve should constantly remember: "Spend less time thinking about what to put in the listener's head. Spend more time thinking about what's already there."

The Myth of Public Speaking

Perhaps at this point you're saying, "How am I to know what's in the brains of those people out there? Most of them are complete strangers to me. I can't read their minds." If this idea dogs you, you may be suffering from what I call *The Myth of Public Speaking.*

The Myth of Public Speaking is the idea that audiences are composed of people who might just as well have wandered in off the street looking for a public rest room. Or perhaps they were passing by the park and saw you speaking atop a soapbox. Maybe they thought listening to you would be more entertaining than feeding the pigeons. Burdened by such misconceptions of how people wind up sitting in audiences, many beginners and practiced voices alike find themselves sinking in a sea of conflicting considerations. The maxim Know Your Listener becomes the impossible dream turned nightmare.

Wake up! The Myth of Public Speaking is just that . . . a myth. With the possible exception of the sidewalk fronting the television store, Hyde Park in London is the *only* forum left in the world where your audience will be composed of people who just *happen* by.

Why Are My Listeners Here?

In the main, people listen to speeches for one or all of the following reasons:

· They are members of the sponsoring organization. Thus, they come to mix with their fellow members and hear about something which relates to their group's purpose.

· An influential person (boss, teacher, spouse) *told* them to be there and "listen-up good."

· They heard about the speech and—owing to the topic or reputation of the speaker—thought it would be stimulating, reassuring, interesting, useful, or entertaining.

· They know you.

In short, the principle of self-selection operates in forming an audience. Of all the ways your listener could have spent his time, he or she *chose* to listen to your speech. The question you must answer is Why? Did they say, "If I go to that speech I may learn something I can use on my job"? Or did they say, "It'll make my wife happy"? Or, "I'll go because City Club luncheons help me understand my community"? Or, "I'll go because Charlie's a friend of mine"?

What Do They Expect of Me?

Figure out why your listeners will come to hear you. Once you do it will be easier to decide what to talk about.

Here's how. Suppose you're an executive with a large paint manufacturer. One day, you are invited to talk to the Sierra Club (a group dedicated to environmental protection and preservation). Without talking to a single member of your future audience you can safely assume that most of your listeners will be there to find out what your company is or is not doing to minimize pollution from its operations. How do you know this? Because that's the purpose of the organization. You can safely bet that they'll be about as interested in your new line of deck stain as in your golf scores. What's more, because many in attendance will be dues-paying *members* of the Sierra Club, you can safely surmise that they share specific beliefs, among them these: that environmental pollution is bad; that manufacturers have a moral and legal obligation to eliminate contaminants from their various discharges; that most companies would sooner pump lead into the ground water than show a quarterly loss; that you, as an employee of the paint company, will defend your employer, right or wrong.

You should certainly double-check all your assumptions about your audience. Once you have, you can anticipate audience reaction to many of your ideas. At the very least, you will know what they want you to talk about. Meeting the test of relevance is the first hurdle in the race to acceptance.

How Much Do They Know?

After learning about their expectations, find out what they know—or *think* they know—about you, about your organization, and about your topic. This will help you decide how much time to spend on the different pieces of your speech as well as to determine its level of complexity. You don't want to waste everyone's time telling them things they already know. Then again, you may find you need to spend time clearing up misconceptions. Or you may find you must convince your listeners that they *need* to know more about a subject in which they currently have no interest.

What Do They Care About?

Let's revisit the Sierra Club. Suppose you've found them well-versed in environmental law, misinformed about your company, but quite knowledgeable about ecological processes. Does this tell you anything about their ages, sexes, occupations, hobbies, religious affiliations, or racial groups? No.

Are these things important? Yes, because if you know

what your listener cares about you can craft your message
to have greater appeal. If our imaginary chapter of the
Sierra Club is loaded with fishing buffs, you'll make points
by talking about how your company's clean-up efforts
brought the trout back to surrounding lakes (assuming this
is true).

How Do They Think?

How do your listeners think? How do they make up their
minds? How receptive are they to new ideas? Tough questions. Since volumes have been written on attitude formation and decision making, this is not the time to write another. Nor is this the place to summarize a hundred years
of psychology. But I would like to give you at least one
example of how knowing a few general facts about your
listeners can tell you a lot about how they'll respond to your
speech.

Risking eighteen years of marital harmony, I will tell you
that women, generally speaking, believe that emotion and
intuition play a greater role in decision making than do
men. For example, if you say your company pioneered the
development of lead-free house paints because the chairman of the board had a niece who was poisoned from eating
peeling paint chips, the women in your audience are more
likely to believe this than the men. Men will tend to greet
this assertion more skeptically. They'll be more likely to
believe that while the story makes for good public relations,
it was really a financial consideration that fostered the development of lead-free paint.

Men say they need more facts and figures in decision
making than do women. Men *do* make decisions based on
their "gut feelings," but are unlikely to do so without having a great store of facts to call upon if challenged.

Further, women tend to be less linear in their reasoning
than men. What do I mean by "less linear"? I mean that

most women aren't as sensitive about the *order* in which information is presented, as long as it's all there. Men usually prefer more systematic presentations where each new piece of information builds on the last.

Finally, women tend to be more empathetic than men; they are more likely to give the speaker the benefit of the doubt. And they are less rigid than men in their thinking about controversial issues.

Are women therefore better listeners than men? No. Apparently, they just have a different *style* of information processing. Are men always going to be more interested than women in topics dealing with facts and figures? No. Remember the principle of self-selection—women attending a speech on tax law are just as likely to be involved in the topic as the men.

Audience Characteristics to Consider

Greater sensitivity to *what* and *how* your listeners think will make you a better speaker. Of course, you must avoid stereotyping and jumping to outlandish conclusions. Still, as speakers, we must continually draw from our experience and make predictions about other people's beliefs and values. The deeper our experience, the better our predictions.

Here are some useful questions to ask the program chair about your listeners:

1. What range of occupations or job titles will be represented?
2. How old will most of them be?
3. Mostly male? Mostly female? Mixed?
4. What racial or ethnic groups will be represented?
5. What are their fears? Heros? Hopes?
6. Is there a dominant religious preference?
7. Will children be present?
8. What political persuasion dominates, if any?

LISTENER SOCIOLOGY

Atmosphere and Customs—Their World and Welcome to It

The difference in atmosphere between the University Faculty Club Luncheon and the Hog Callers' Barbecue will be as striking as between Mt. Everest and New Orleans. The former might be cold and testing, the latter warm and forgiving. Your approach to any speech should take atmosphere into account.

Customs and taboos are also important. Rotarians, for example, frown on speakers who use their platform to make a sales pitch. Even fifteen seconds of self-promotion within an otherwise altruistic speech will be considered ill-mannered, disrespectful of the club's purpose (to serve the community).

Unfortunately, organizations rarely take the initiative to explain their ways to outsiders. You must discover them for yourself. Do this by talking with current members. One question that always yields useful information is this one: "What would I have to do to be told *never* to return?" The answer might be, "Speak longer than your allotted time." Or it might be, "Refuse to wear the antlers given to you at the door."

Some customs and rituals may seem silly to you. But remember, a speech is normally *just one* act of a larger play; the play may be tightly scripted, like a national political convention, or loosely scripted, like a neighborhood meeting.

Whatever the rules of the host organization, obey them as far as conscience will allow. Show respect for your hosts. If people sense a lack of respect, they won't listen.

So go ahead. Wear the antlers. And smile.

The Lens of Culture

Your listener's perceptions of you and your presentation will be filtered through the lens of culture. Because culture varies with locale and time, the facts I have chosen to illustrate cultural bias may not be facts where or when you read this book.

Audio-Visual Sophistication

Never have visual delights been so plentiful. Eye-popping graphics are commonplace; they illustrate the six o'clock news, animate computer games, and turn the lowly cereal box into a poor man's Rembrandt. Colorful, sharp, artistically sophisticated visual materials are the rule, not the exception.

Accustomed to this high-style visual bombardment, we expect quality in the visual materials used by speakers. If you show your listeners hastily prepared, sloppy visual materials, the believability of your ideas will likely be reduced, not enhanced.

Audiences expect good sound and staging as well. The entertainment industry and the White House—assisted by the most advanced equipment and talent money can buy—have raised our expectations for every variety of performance and presentation. Malfunctioning microphones, cheesy decorations, interruptions by stage hands, glaring sunlight—all these tend to annoy people deeply.

We'll talk more about the use and abuse of visual materials in chapter 5.

Busy Living

Most people are extraordinarily busy these days, holding a job and/or attending school, taking care of home and family, and getting away to relax when they can. We have little time to hem and haw. We grow impatient quickly. We want speakers to move their ideas forward and get to the point. Don't fight it. Just do it. You want your audience to be with you, not ahead of you.

Egocentricity

Looking out for them and theirs—that's how most people spend their time these days. Speakers must work diligently to prove that their ideas *matter* to their listeners.

Cynicism

Late-twentieth-century Americans are cynical about the doings of public officials and business executives. And they are not cowed by the trappings of high office. Accordingly, speakers in high places are wise to heavily edit their speeches—not just for accuracy, but for plausibility as well.

Confusion about Authority

We want our speechmakers to be smart and powerful. Otherwise, why should we bother listening? But at the same time, we want them to be *like us*—fallible, sometimes confused, and occasionally at a loss for words.

Infomania

Each day it rains facts and numbers, fallout from modernity. Bank statements, opinion polls, telephone numbers, access codes, performance statistics, zip codes, and how the list goes on. No matter what our station in life, numbers and statistics crowd it.

Already stuffed with facts, the last thing most of us want from a speech is another heaping helping. Consequently, our fact-glutted age places a premium on perspective and discounts the value of raw data.

TYPICAL SPEECH SETTINGS

When you are asked to give a speech, it will likely be one of eight kinds: a sales presentation, an address to a service club, a banquet speech, a convention or conference presentation, a business presentation to management, testimony at a public meeting, a political speech, or a talk before a student audience. Each of these varieties is discussed below, but only for the purpose of orientation. Accordingly, these discussions are very brief, except one— the sales presentation. Because more people are concerned about this than the others, it deserves our immediate and close attention. While we're mapping the sales presentation, many topics covered extensively in later chapters are bound to loom into view. These chapters will be referenced as they come up.

The Sales Presentation

An easy proficiency with the sales presentation is a wonderful skill to have. It can also be a job requirement of the first magnitude. But for the novice, it is much more. One's first sales presentation is a rite of passage into capitalism.

Like all ritual, the sales pitch has its own mythology, complete with epic stories and legendary heroes, each leaving to future generations a revised edition of *The Seventy-Five Most Effective Closes of the Master Salesman.* All this tends to intimidate and confuse the neophyte.

Most people are relieved to discover that a good sales presentation can be created by following a simple, time-tested pattern. It's one of many used for speeches to persuade and activate (see chapters 2 and 10). You'll probably recognize it from your own experience as a customer. The examples I've selected to illustrate the basic pattern have been deliberately chosen not for elegance, but for raw simplicity.

Example 1

One cold winter evening many years ago, I was a college student home on break looking for a way to make some fast money. My search led me to a small room where I waited with ten or so other young men to apply for a job selling vacuum cleaners door-to-door. We'd all answered an ad in the paper and none of us was quite prepared for what happened next.

A fastidious, earnest man in a white suit stepped out from behind a curtain, looked us over intently and said essentially this:

"Good evening, gentlemen. I'm glad you could make it. My name is Mr. Gregory. My business cards say I'm the Regional Vice President for Sales and Marketing. But my salespeople just call me Greg. That's because I didn't always have business cards and a big title. Two years ago I was sitting where you're sitting. I was skeptical. I was a little nervous, maybe even scared. But there was no doubt whatsoever that I was flat broke. I was ready to try anything. As you see, the risk paid off.

"I say this because I know you came here tonight looking for one thing. Here it is. [He pulled a sheaf of currency from his pocket and fanned it out.] Call it dough, call it money, call it the root of all evil, it's what you don't have enough of and that's why you're willing to sit here tonight and listen to what I'm about to tell you.

"Let me start by saying I think you all deserve a chance to make more money. You're all sharp-looking guys and you should have that new car, that hot date on Saturday night, that house or education or whatever it is you're after. You deserve it as much as anybody else. Am I right?

"So whaddaya gonna do? Well, you can pump gas and

you can sell shoes. But I'll tell you something. You won't make any money. Maybe a hundred dollars a week, tops. And what kind of dough is that for a guy with ambition? It's nothing. Sure, you can *survive* on it, but you can't *live* on it. [See chapter 4 on starting a speech.]

"Let me ask you a question. How much do you think a person can make showing carpet maintenance equipment to homeowners in your neighborhood? Two hundred dollars a week? Three hundred dollars? Four hundred dollars? You're getting warmer, but you're not close. A thousand dollars a week. You heard me right. Not a thousand a month. A thousand a week. Think of what you could do with a thousand a week. [See chapter 9 on rhetorical questions.]

"I'm not going to insult your intelligence by telling you that every one of our guys makes that much. The average is closer to six hundred dollars a week—six times what you'll make in that shoe store. But you don't have to take that from me. Ask Ron here. He's one of our guys. Ron, how much did you make last month? [Ron says eight hundred dollars a week.] There it is, gentlemen. You guessed right. You *can* make good money presenting our carpet maintenance equipment to our prequalified buyers. [See chapter 4 on supporting your ideas.]

"How is it done? I'll show you exactly how it's done. [He pulled a spotless vacuum cleaner from behind the curtain.] This is the Suction King, and as you'll see, gentlemen, it does more than clean. It virtually sells itself." (See chapter 6 on visual aids and props.)

And with no shame whatsoever, Mr. Gregory poured a cup of ashes over a beige carpet sample and proceeded to vacuum it up. When he finished, he continued.

"How many of you thought that was a cheap stunt? Good. Because it was. Any vacuum on the market today can do that. But here's what they can't do."

Mr. Gregory smoothly replaced the filter in the Suction

King, walked over to what looked to everyone like a perfectly clean rug and began vacuuming. After a few seconds, he removed the filter and passed it around the group. It was filthy—covered with dirt and hair that the Suction King had mysteriously extracted from the seemingly clean carpet.

"And that, gentlemen," crowed Mr. Gregory, "is what sells the Suction King."

After trotting out some statistics proving that the Suction King would pay for itself in foregone steam-cleaning bills, Mr. Gregory paused, then drove it home.

"You've seen how easy it is to sell our product. And you've met people who've made good money doing it. You can do it too. But please don't hesitate to seize this opportunity. You don't have to be broke and feeling your life is going nowhere. Do something about it now. We still have openings for motivated salespeople tonight. Tomorrow we may not. I can't guarantee you a spot on our team tomorrow.

"If you're interested in taking charge of your life—and I think you are—come on up here now. That's right. Just come on up. Sign this employment guarantee and Mr. Robbins here will set you up with everything you need to be out making money as early as tomorrow afternoon." (See chapter 4 on speeches to activate.)

That was it.

This pitch may seem bullying, unsophisticated, or condescending. But Mr. Gregory knew what he was doing. It worked. While he didn't enlist me (he didn't allay my fears of humiliation), he did sign several eager recruits, their pride eroded by desperation.

His pattern of presentation followed a classic formula.

Standard Sales Pitch Formula

Step 1. Make the customer aware that he or she has an immediate problem or unfulfilled need.

Step 2. Present the customer with a way to solve the problem or satisfy the need.

Step 3. Overcome the customer's stated or unstated objections to the solution you propose.

Step 4. Establish (or reinforce) the urgency of the problem.

Step 5. Ask the customer for the order (signature on purchase order, shipping approval, verbal acceptance of the solution, or whatever).

Example 2

Despite vast differences in setting, item sold, and audience, this next presentation follows the same pattern as the previous example.

The pitch was made on a weekly television program about new products in the field of personal computers. The salesperson worked for a respected software company. His product was a program designed to locate and restore data which has become lost to the operator through any of a number of possible malfunctions. Anyone who works on a computer worries about this.

The pitch was simple. The salesman first reminded us how irreplaceable data can be easily lost on the average home and office computer through simple mechanical and electrical malfunctions. He then displayed a computer system which had suffered such a loss of memory. No matter how hard he worked the keyboard, he was unable to get the computer to retrieve the errant bits and bytes. Then he revealed his product—an ordinary looking software diskette carrying a magical program. The program would, he said, find the lost data and bring it back to our fingertips. In went the diskette and five keystrokes later the lost data was raised from the dead. Lest we had forgotten, the salesman reminded us that such potentially devastating computer glitches can happen to anyone at any time. He then stressed that his program was an easy-to-use, inexpensive alternative to re-creating lost data from scratch. He concluded by asking interested viewers to call their local software dealer for more information.

The software pitch and the recruiting pitch followed the same pattern. Both began by focusing on the customer's problem, the problem the item was designed to solve. "You have no money and you can't make enough the usual way," said the vacuum sales recruiter. As for the software pitch, the problem was the computer user's vulnerability to data loss. After this, a solution is presented; the viability of the solution is established; the seriousness and urgency of the problem are restated; and finally, the customer is asked to buy.

Sales Presentations Operate on Two Levels

Like all speeches to persuade, sales presentations operate on at least two levels. These levels are like multiple tracks on a complex recording. Played together, the tracks make the music.

Our examples highlighted only one of these tracks: the argument track. This is the logical progression of ideas and facts which leads from problem to solution. But by itself, it is not enough. To keep the customer *receptive* to the argument track, the salesperson must lay down another: the confidence track.

The confidence track is mostly nonverbal, but not entirely. It keeps the customer involved in the sales encounter and does this in several ways. First, the confidence track regulates the pace of the argument track. It can be fast, as with anonymous telephone solicitations. Or slow, as with sales dependent on personal relationships built over a period of months or years. Second, the confidence track in-

cludes "trust me" signals: comments and actions which tell
the listener, "I know your problems and I'm here to help
you." The vacuum recruiter's comment that he too was
once an applicant was part of the confidence track. Third,
in a face-to-face sales encounter the confidence track also
includes the salesperson's body language, vocal style, and
clothing. Experienced salespeople will attempt to impercep-
tibly mimic the gestures, accent, and clothing style of the
customer. They do this to lessen distractions and boost their
likability. This all helps keep the customer riding smoothly
along the argument track to the close of the sale. (See
chapter 8 on effective delivery.)

No matter what the setting, product, or audience, the
basic pattern is effective. The formula itself is firmly rooted
in the salesperson's imperative: "You gotta make 'em want
it." Your chances of making 'em want it will greatly improve through good audience analysis.

The Service Club Lunch

A vast mouthful of public speaking in America occurs at
Rotary, Lions, Kiwanis, and a myriad other service and
community clubs. Meetings are usually held on weekdays
between 12 noon and 2 PM. Most listeners will be men
between the ages of thirty and sixty-five. The typical agenda
calls for a business meeting conducted through lunch, followed by the "program" (the speaker's slot). The business
meeting itself is likely to include a report on the club's
current project(s), the induction of new members, the recognition of visiting members from out-of-town clubs, and
short reports on various items of interest to the member-
ship. Service club meetings are commonly held in local
restaurants, hotel meeting rooms, or, if the group is large
enough, in the banquet hall of a convention center or hotel.

Because many members must return to work, meetings must end promptly. It is normal for the invited speaker to have his or her time shrunk by an overly ambitious agenda. And since the main speaker is usually last, they are pressured the most to end on time. Speakers at service clubs must cope with a variety of distractions and obstacles: rattling tableware, minds numbed by digestion, entering and exiting members, and more.

The Banquet Speech

If you speak at a banquet, the key word is *enjoyment.* Banquets are held to bring people together and have fun. That they sometimes fall short of the mark is often the fault of event planners who overestimate the endurance of the celebrants and underestimate the duration of the speeches. Odds are, you'll speak from a lectern placed at the center of a head table. Speeches take place after dinner so you'll likely be on deck somewhere between 7:30 and 10:00 PM. That's late. People will be tired. Odds are they will have been drinking. Keep it short and lively. In the course of the evening, your listeners are destined to hear too many speakers, observe the presentation of too many awards, and hear "It's my great honor and privilege" with excruciating frequency. Still, whether you introduce an award winner, receive an award, or make the keynote address, banquet speaking offers unlimited opportunity for fun. Take full advantage.

The Convention or Conference Presentation

The good news first: Your listeners will be there because they are truly interested in your topic (as described in the convention program guide). Because most conventions have several optional events going on simultaneously, you may get two listeners, or you may get five hundred. It depends on your competition. Odds are, most of your listeners will be strangers—to you and to each other. Unless you're the first speaker to use the room, you may find it a mess when you arrive. Chairs and coffee cups may be scattered about. Your lectern may be missing. And so on. Get there early to fix up the place. This is especially important if microphones or audiovisual (AV) equipment are needed. The person you'll need for AV repairs may take quite a while to find. This alone is a good reason not to plan a multimedia extravaganza.

The energy level of conventioneers hits a peak with the keynote address (usually on the first or second night) and drops from there. If you speak in the 11 AM slot of a convention ending that day at 12 noon, expect the few in attendance to have their bags with them. Also, early morning slots are tough because people are worn out from travel and/or partying the night before. The best slots for informative and persuasive speeches are in the midmorning hours.

Presentations to Management

What you'll face will vary greatly with the culture of your organization. Because the stakes can be high, you *must* research the situation you'll enter by talking with coworkers who've already been there. Does Jones listen well, or does she doodle? How much does Atkins already know about my project? Will anyone there be vigorously opposed? Will they ask me questions when I'm done, or just show me out?

Generally, the worst mistakes to make are being late, going overtime, being sloppily or unsuitably dressed, and not knowing what you're talking about. Most business executives expect good organization, relevant material, and crisp presentation. Because few decisions are made individually these days, you will likely be talking to three or more people. Some in attendance may be rivals for a higher position. Even if not, be prepared for arguments to spring up among your listeners. Let the boss settle them. Your job is just to give the facts as you know them.

Legislative Hearings and Public Meetings

Legislative bodies—city councils, state and federal legislative committees, and the like—often hold public hearings to get citizen input. The legislators and members of their staffs will sit ceremoniously up front in a big room and hear the opinions of their constituents. Typically, a notice will be published listing the date, time, and place of the hearings. At the meeting hall you will find a sign-up sheet or other such device to schedule interested speakers. Speakers are normally limited to a short comment period—three to five minutes—unless they represent a larger constituency. Odds are, you will have to wait a long time to speak. Exactly *when* you speak will be determined by your position on the list as well as by how much talking the legislators or officials do between speakers.

The public officials and legislators who make up your principal audience may show no signs whatsoever of listening to a word you say. Their heads may be buried in paperwork. They may be reading the newspaper. They may be chatting with their spouses on the phone. All the while, the clock ticks away against your allotment. Speak your piece well, forcefully, and respectfully. Don't take your listeners' antics seriously. Legislators develop an uncanny ability to hear what's important while otherwise engaged. What's important is votes, power, money, and the public welfare. In that order.

If your speech openly attacks the merits of an earlier legislative action, be prepared for a withering counterattack by an indignant official. Stand your ground. In America at least, they can't put you in jail for expressing your views at a public meeting.

Political Events

Political meetings are held for four main purposes. First, to raise money. Second, to build support for the party's current slate of candidates and/or legislative proposals. Third, to malign the opposition. And fourth, to raise money.

Typically, they are low-rent affairs. Every penny spent on pretzels for the faithful is a penny better spent on ammunition (direct mail solicitations, yard signs, TV and radio spots) and candidate support (hotel bills, airfare, room service breakfasts with fat cats and media advisors).

As a speaker at a political rally, your first concern is lung power. Your second, enthusiasm. Your third, the possibility of becoming overheated.

Most importantly, your listeners expect to hear something noteworthy about the ideals, purposes, dangers, or opportunities of government. Odds are good that they will be dissatisfied if your speech is merely a partisan diatribe.

School Audiences

It's not easy being a kid—especially for a forty year old with high blood pressure and a second mortgage. So it's best not to try.

Remember that schools are run by the clock. The normal class period for kids thirteen and up is forty minutes. Let's suppose you're the invited guest for an entire class period.

Allow ten minutes for the teacher to bring the class to order
and introduce you. Allow ten minutes of awkward silence
for questions after you talk. That leaves you about twenty
minutes to get in big trouble with the school board.

Truth aside, kids are wonderful to talk to. But as with
legislators, expect their listening behavior to be refresh-
ingly honest.

2

DECIDE WHAT YOU WANT TO ACHIEVE

WHY GIVE A SPEECH?

For many years I worked as an on-call speechwriter. When a client had to give a speech, I'd be summoned and together we'd discuss the assignment and thrash out the main ideas. I'd then go home and write the first draft. While none of this was easy, I remember one client meeting as being particularly difficult. My client, an accomplished, studious man in his fifties, was not cooperating. When I asked a specific question, he'd answer in generalities. When I asked for clarification, he'd refer me to a journal article. After thirty minutes I still had no clear idea of what he wanted his speech to be about or accomplish. All else having failed, I tried an indirect approach. I said, "George, imagine you've just finished your speech. You're standing there preparing to leave the stage. Right then, what do you want your listeners to be thinking?" George said, "I want them to be thinking, 'That guy George is the smartest S.O.B. I ever heard.'"

I said, "OK, fine. But what will make them say that?"
And George said, "They'll say it when I show them how to
deliver higher quality service by spending less, instead of
more."

"Great, now we're getting somewhere."

George's primary goal was to be admired by his colleagues. This goal was a personal one. Personal goals are
what we hope to accomplish *for ourselves* by giving speeches.

George's secondary goal was to persuade his listeners
that they could lower their costs and still improve the quality of their services. This was his *communication goal.* Communication goals describe how we want to affect the beliefs,
feelings, or attitudes of our listeners. Our communication
goals are usually, but not always, different from our personal goals. For example, a school board member gives a
speech on public education finance. His communication
goal is to persuade his listeners that his plan will result in
lower taxes and better schools. Is this his personal goal as
well? Perhaps so if the speech is his farewell address. But
what if he gives it during a run for reelection? Then the
odds say his personal goal is to get reelected.

Personal goals supply ultimate reasons why people give
speeches. They supply the passion. Without passion, spirit,
or desire, there is only this and that. But a speech lacking
a clear communication goal is either an exercise in self-
indulgence or a muddle—not worth doing in either case.

FIVE KINDS OF SPEECHES
TO REACH FIVE
COMMUNICATION GOALS

To stimulate, to inform, to persuade, to activate, and to
entertain—these are the five kinds of speeches commonly
recognized by veteran speech makers.

The Speech to Stimulate

> I have nothing to offer but blood, toil, tears and sweat. . . . You ask, what is our policy. I say it is to wage war by land, sea, and air. War with all our might and with all the strength God has given us, and to wage war against a monstrous tyranny never surpassed in the dark and lamentable catalogue of human crime.
>
> You ask, what is our aim. I can answer in one word. It is victory. Victory at all costs—victory in spite of all terrors—victory. . . .
>
> —WINSTON CHURCHILL'S *first speech to parliament upon appointment as prime minister, May 13, 1940.* [1]

> I have a dream that one day on the red hills of Georgia the sons of former slaves and the sons of former slave owners will be able to sit down together at the table of brotherhood.
>
> I have a dream that one day even the state of Mississippi, a desert state sweltering with the heat of injustice and oppression, will be transformed into an oasis of freedom and justice.
>
> I have a dream that my four little children will one day live in a nation where they will not be judged by the color of their skin but by the content of their character.
>
> I have a dream today.
>
> —DR. MARTIN LUTHER KING, JR., *from his speech at the civil rights march on Washington, D.C., August 28, 1963.* [2]

Churchill's speech had an immediate, intense effect on the soul of Britain. Rushing feelings of patriotic pride were bonded to the will to survive. Martin Luther King also sought to arouse the passions of his listeners. But the passions King hoped to generate were not those needed to promote physical survival, but those necessary for spiritual survival: the longing for justice and the quest for love and acceptance.

The *pure* speech to stimulate seeks only to reinforce and

intensify feelings that are already resident in the listener. If those feelings are ready for a push, so much the better. Times of war and unrest, not surprisingly, offer the best examples of effective speaking to stimulate. But we should not overlook the fact that speeches to stimulate hold great importance in our everyday affairs: for example, when the drama coach speaks to the cast before opening night or when the sales manager pulls the sales force in from the field to generate enthusiasm for a new product line.

When my speech is over, I want my listener to feel. . . .

The Speech to Inform

> I decided to entitle my talk today "The Five Major Risks of Academic High Achievement." An alternative and slightly broader title might be: "Five Ways in Which Thinking Is Dangerous."
> Way number one, it seems to me, is that thinking—analysis—the habit of probing deeply into things—can lead to depression. . . .
> A second risk of academic high achievement is that there are those who will actually hold it against you. . . .
>
> —STEVEN JOEL TRACHTENBERG, *president, University of Hartford, in a speech to Newington High School Scholars, June 3, 1986.* [3]

> My intent today is, first, to provide an overview of the global economy, with particular attention to the third world. And then to focus on four economic issues that deserve priority attention in 1984. . . . These issues are: improving economic policy and performance in the industrial countries; liberalizing trade; reviving international capital flows; and improving economic policy in the developing countries.
>
> —A. W. CLAUSEN, *president, World Bank, in a speech to the European Management Forum, January 26, 1984.* [4]

Examples of speeches to inform are easy to find. But as we'll see in chapter 4, examples of *well-executed* ones are not. Whether well done or raw, informative speeches are nonetheless the staple of contemporary speech making, standard fare from classroom to board room, from lecture hall to town hall forum. Open any urban newspaper and you'll find notices of public lectures on everything from lowering your tax bill to lowering your blood pressure; from raising peacocks to raising the dead. All are speeches to inform. Until, that is, they encourage purchase of the book, cassette, and videotape which explain the whole matter in greater detail. At that point, they become speeches to persuade and activate.

What the forehand volley is to tennis, the speech to inform is to speech making. It is fundamental. Those who can do it well are much more likely to succeed at the game than those who can not.

When my speech is over, I want my listeners to know that. . . .

The Speech to Persuade

> I speak to you because small children need big friends. Young children need older advocates who will plead in favor of meeting their needs, speak up for them because they can not speak for themselves. They have not lived long enough to be politically sophisticated, only long enough to be abused and neglected.
>
> —BOB KEESHAN, *"Captain Kangaroo," in a speech to CityClub, Seattle, April 13, 1988.* [5]

Famine was once a normal part of [life]. Since A.D. 10, what is now the United Kingdom has experienced 180 famines; between 106 B.C. and 1929 China endured 1,828 famines, an average of 90 per century. Twelve percent of the Irish population was wiped out by famine less than 150 years ago.

But now, today, famine is not—I repeat NOT—a normal part of the human condition. As reported in the authoritative *Science* magazine . . .

> —RICHARD F. SCHUBERT, *President, American Red Cross, in a speech to the Charleston Rotary Club, March 11, 1988.* [6]

Market share. Strategic planning. Product lines. The jargon of business and the marketplace has invaded the health care field. . . .

No one has proven that this "more business-like environment" has led to higher quality or less costly delivery. . . .

Unrestrained competition in health care is basically incompatible with the ethical basis of medicine. It coerces health care providers into placing financial concerns and interests above concern for individual patients.

> —RON J. ANDERSON, *Chairman of the Texas Board of Health, speaking in Dallas, Texas, April 21, 1986.* [7]

The speech to persuade expresses a viewpoint and works to prove it. In some persuasive speeches the viewpoint is stated directly. But most often and most unfortunately, the speaker will not state the point directly, instead assuming it is clear from the "overall context of the remarks"—or some other such nonsense.

The examples quoted above are rare and refreshing. There's no mistaking what the speakers seek to prove. Keeshan hopes to convince adults to fight for the rights and futures of children. Schubert aims to convince his audience that famines are not normal, inevitable, or acceptable. Anderson seeks to persuade us that free-market capitalism and sound medical practice don't mix.

Persuading is more than informing. Informing someone of the high cancer rates among cigarette smokers is not the same as persuading them that smoking will probably give them cancer. Just ask the surgeon general. When we say we've persuaded someone, what we usually mean is that *now* they believe something they didn't believe before. With people who know little and have no competing beliefs, persuasion can be simply a matter of supplying new information. For example, when children are told that Santa Claus comes down the chimney on Christmas eve to bring them presents, they believe. Why not? It's an attractive idea. And, for the two year old, nearly anything is possible. But as we grow older, we learn things. And many of the things we learn actually strengthen our beliefs in things which are not true. This makes it hard for the persuader to persuade—even when armed with great volumes of otherwise convincing information. Albert Einstein, the greatest physicist of our time, fought vigorously to repudiate quantum theory, despite plentiful evidence that it was true.

Our resistance to new ideas is sometimes caused by other beliefs for which we have seemingly solid evidence. Other times, resistance derives from the habit of believing and saying the opposite. Racial prejudices develop this way. And the resistance of prejudice is agonizingly difficult to overcome.

Persuasion, then, is usually a task of overcoming the resistance of other ideas and old habits, not merely a task of supplying new information.

When my speech is over, I want my listeners to believe that. . . .

The Speech to Activate

As soon as we get thirty callers, we'll end this pledge drive and return to our regular programming. Just think, you can speed that up.

And remember, you pay for your newspaper to get your

news. Why shouldn't you likewise support this station which brings you hours of insightful news coverage on the air. It's the right thing to do. It's the fair thing to do. So do the right thing. Call. Right now. 543-9595. And pledge your support for public radio. Give ten dollars a month and we'll dedicate an entire day of listening to the friend of your choice. Pledge twenty dollars per month and we'll give you a free stay at a lovely bed and breakfast hotel. All you have to do is call 543-9595. Please do it now.

—*Announcer, KUOW Public Radio, Seattle, September 27, 1988.*

O sinner! consider the fearful danger you are in. 'Tis a great furnace of wrath, a wide and bottomless pit, full of fire and wrath, that you are held over in the hand of God. . . . You hang by a slender thread, with the flames of divine wrath flashing about it. . . .

Therefore let everyone that is out of Christ now awake and fly from the wrath to come. The wrath of Almighty God is now undoubtedly hanging over a great part of his congregation. Let everyone fly out of Sodom. "Haste and escape for your lives, look not behind you, escape to the mountain, lest ye be consumed."

—JONATHAN EDWARDS, *in a sermon delivered in Enfield, Connecticut, July 8, 1741.*[8]

The speech to activate wants people to *do* something. This is *not* the same thing as persuading. It is more. The speech to activate takes the additional step of telling the listener, in effect, "Now that you're convinced, do this." Many speakers mistakenly believe that once a person is convinced, she or he will automatically act. Life proves otherwise. Many a voter, convinced that Jones is the better candidate, shuns the polling booth on voting day. Many a true believer puts no money in the collection box. Many a manager believes that excessive stress impairs the performance of workers, yet does nothing to relieve the pressure. Countless speeches to activate fail because the speakers are not *specific* about what they want the listener to do. In the examples above, both speakers sought action. But while the KUOW pitchman was very specific, Edwards was not. The pitchman didn't say "Support public radio." He said, call *this* number. Pledge *this* amount. And do it *now*. By contrast, Edwards used a metaphor to ask his listeners to lead a more virtuous life—whatever that is. The Jonathan Edwardses of our day would never consider ending such a sermon so ambiguously. Instead, they say, "*Come* forward now. *Sign* the pledge card. *Kneel* down with one of my staff. *Pray* for Christ to enter your life today."

When I finish my speech, I want my listeners to do the following. . . .

The Speech to Entertain

President Butler paid me a compliment a while ago in mentioning my name in his introductory remarks, and he put me ahead of the Columbia graduates. I'm glad he did that, because I got the worst of it last week. The Prince of Wales last week, in speaking of the sights of America, mentioned the Woolworth Building, the subway, the slaughterhouse, Will Rogers, and the Ford Factory. He could at least have put me ahead of the hogs.

Everything must be in contrast at an affair like this. You know, to show anything off properly you must have the contrast. Now, I am here tonight representing poverty. We have enough wealth right here at this table, right here at this speaker's table alone so that we could liquidate the national debt. Every rich man reaches a time in his career when he comes to a turning point and starts to give it away. I have heard that of several of our guests here tonight, and that is one of the reasons that I am here. I would like to be here at the psychological moment.

—WILL ROGERS, *in an after-dinner speech to Columbia University Alumni, New York City, December 4, 1924.* [9]

Gentlemen: I reverently believe that the Maker who made us all, makes everything in New England—but the weather. I don't know who makes that, but I think it must be raw apprentices in the Weather Clerk's factory, who experiment and learn how in New England for board and clothes and then are promoted to make weather for countries that require a good article and will take their business elsewhere if they don't get it.

    —MARK TWAIN *(Samuel Clemens), in an after-dinner speech to the New England Society, December 22, 1876.* [10]

When it comes to graduation speeches, it is generally concluded that time—a generous dollop of time—is of the essence.

This is because the chief function of the graduation speaker has always been to prevent graduating seniors from being released into the real world before they've been properly sedated.

Like all anesthetics, graduation speeches take time to kick in, so I'm going to ask you to bear with me for about a quarter of an hour. It will go faster if you think of it as the equivalent of four videos.

    —GARRY TRUDEAU, *cartoonist, in a commencement address at Wake Forest University, May 19, 1986.* [11]

Speeches to entertain are usually humorous from start to finish. Still, they differ from mere joke telling in the same way that playing a baseball game differs from batting practice. In both, you try to hit the ball, but in the game, it's one part of a larger effort.

So it goes with entertaining speeches. They use the vehicle of comedy (in any or all of its forms) to speed the listener down a parkway of persuasion. Ronald Reagan, actor and popular two-term president, understood the persuasive role of humor and used it to great effect. Before people knew it, they'd laughed themselves into voting for nearly everything he proposed.

Speaking to entertain is tough work. In 1981 I took a

class on speech writing from Dr. Jerry Tarver, Professor of Speech Communication at the University of Richmond. After giving a thoroughly entertaining presentation on the various kinds of speeches, this modest man said, "I think I'd rather have a baby than give a speech to entertain."

Humorous speaking is so difficult that even those to whom funny business comes naturally think twice before committing premeditated humor. Only the prospect of bankruptcy from a disastrous business venture could force Twain onto the after-dinner circuit. Spontaneous humor is one thing. Planned mirth is another.

The difficulty, importance, and popularity of humor in speaking justify giving it a chapter of its own—chapter 11.

While I give my speech, I want my listeners to be amused, entertained, happy.

WHEN TO GIVE WHICH KIND OF SPEECH

Congratulations. You've just read the most important pages of this book. If you believe every speech should be designed to achieve a definite goal and if you understand the difference between the five kinds of speeches, you are miles ahead of your competition.

The next problem is when to use which one. There are no ironclad rules, but some ideas may help.

1. *Consider your own abilities.*   It is more difficult to give a successful persuasive speech than to give a successful speech to inform. By degree of difficulty from least to most, I would rank the kinds of speeches this way: to inform, to stimulate, to persuade, to activate, to entertain.

Why this order of difficulty? Some reasons are simple.

Before you can persuade someone of something, you have to inform them of what it is. Likewise, before you can get someone to do something, you have to persuade them it's the right thing to do. Further, there's the element of time. Accomplishing one task in twenty minutes is easier than accomplishing that and two more. The speaker usually has the same allotment of time (usually fifteen to twenty-five minutes), no matter what his or her goal. Consequently, the speaker must be more efficient at each task.

Some people find it easy to give speeches to stimulate, but have trouble with the regimentation required for the speeches to inform, persuade, and activate. The tasks of outlining and culling research materials leave them cold.

Then again, giving a Winston Churchill–quality speech to stimulate will be infinitely harder for the average speaker than pulling off a straightforward speech to persuade. And some of us, myself included, must flog ourselves mercilessly to get sufficiently lathered up to give a good pep talk.

Finally, if you've ever attempted one, you know better than to underestimate the difficulty of speeches to entertain.

2. *Don't preach to the choir.*   If the locals have already been converted, do your missionary work in another village.

3. *Consider the mood of your listeners.*   A funeral is no place for a speech to entertain; better a speech to stimulate feelings of love and hope. An after-dinner audience of tipsy conventioneers is likewise no place for a persuasive address because late-hour listeners usually lack the ability and will to concentrate.

4. *For experienced speakers:*   Stretch yourself when you can. If you're in a rut giving the same old speech to inform,

get out of it. Challenge yourself. Use the next appropriate opportunity to persuade your audience of something that follows from all that information you've been dispensing. The chance to try something new will not come by often. When it does, take it.

3

SELECTING YOUR TOPIC

The title of this chapter may seem ill-chosen. Many beginning speakers believe they have no power whatsoever when it comes to selecting the topic of their talk. They feel compelled to accept whatever title, subject matter, and general direction is suggested by those issuing the invitation.

Don't be. As speaker, you have every right—and every responsibility as well—to determine what you say and how you say it. The purpose of this chapter is to help you choose a topic that will please both you and your audience.

Five Rules

RULE 1—*Choose a Topic That Suits the Occasion*

A Tale of Two Topics

I was first struck by the room—huge, yellow, and empty but for a single podium and at least two thousand chairs. In half an hour it would house the keynote speech for the 1985

American Psychological Association convention. That summer this was the largest convention in the country, with 15,000 brainy people scattered throughout a hundred or so meeting rooms in downtown Los Angeles.

Every seat was filled fifteen minutes before the speech. Those who couldn't find a chair lined the walls and sat in the aisles, wheelchairs up front. Savants traded stories about the great man soon to appear while the rest of us fed from the kinetic energy, wondering what would happen next.

Right on schedule, the man we'd come to see took to the platform. He was all forehead on a body of articulated matchsticks. Dressed in a dark suit, he seemed to be on stilts. And he was old—some people said eighty. You could feel the worry that he might not make it to the podium or have the voice to manage the crowd. We were reassured by the presence of the youthful man at his side. His introduction soon completed, the old man straightened and took his place behind the podium.

Then a frightening thing happened. A disheveled man rushed in from a side exit. He was angry, and nuts. Ranting and raving, he crossed to center stage and stopped in front of the podium. He turned toward the speaker, shouting nonsense and jerking all about. The great man didn't flinch, he just looked at this fellow as he would a pigeon pecking on his window sill, eyes following with detached interest as security people hauled the intruder away.

When the disturbance had cleared, the legend looked at all of us and said: "The title of my talk today is, What Is Wrong with Daily Life in the Western World."

Nobody laughed. The speaker was B. F. Skinner, one of the most influential and controversial psychologists since Sigmund Freud.

In Contrast:

It was May 9, 1970. Angry crowds had surrounded the Washington Monument and Lincoln Memorial in Washington, D.C., to protest the United States' military invasion of Cambodia. The Defense Department called it a retaliatory incursion. The protestors called it an outrage, another unlawful expansion of an unlawful war—the Vietnam conflict. They demanded an explanation. They wanted to know why President Richard Nixon had ordered the invasion. But moreover, they wanted to tell him to stop it. Five days earlier, four students protesting the Cambodian operation were shot and killed by troops of the Ohio National Guard.

Under intense pressure from all quarters of society to get U.S. forces out of Southeast Asia, and fearing the prospect of the evening news showing D.C. riot police teargassing citizens at the Washington Monument, President Nixon decided in the early hours of the morning to visit protestors at the Lincoln Memorial.

Stooped from exhaustion, Nixon trudged up the steps of the memorial, approached a group of young people and began rambling on about football and surfing. The president of Vanderbilt University remarked later on this bizarre occurrence, saying that to talk with students about surfing and football so soon after the Kent State shootings was like "telling a joke at a funeral."[12]

The Lesson

Skinner chose a big topic for a big occasion. Nixon chose an irrelevant topic for a momentous occasion. No doubt Nixon had a reason for what he did. We might plausibly guess he wanted to relieve tension by changing the subject. It didn't work—it only made him appear disconnected and insensitive.

Ask yourself, "Why do they want *me*? What is it that I know, do, or represent that makes *me* the one they want?" Ask yourself, "What are they expecting me to do, to say?" The best speeches satisfy, then exceed expectations.

RULE 2—*Choose a Topic That You Can Credibly Address*

Only someone with the stature of B. F. Skinner could credibly describe what is wrong with daily life in the western world—let alone do it in twenty-five minutes. I should immediately add that your credibility is not merely a function of how learned a speech you give. A public relations executive once complained to me about her client, a tax accountant. It seems her client wanted desperately to expand his customer list by giving speeches about global economics to wealthy business leaders. Of course, he wanted his P.R. exec to write the speech and secure the bookings. His strategy was pitifully flawed from the start. Few of his targeted listeners would consider a tax accountant an expert on global economic theory—no matter how brilliant his speechwriter.

RULE 3—*Choose a Fresh Topic, or a Fresh Perspective*

If you've been passing your time weaving blankets in a Mongolian yurt, you *may* not have heard that (1) health care costs are taking up an ever-larger share your budget, (2) the technology of medicine is growing increasingly sophisticated and more expensive to buy and operate, and (3) American society is aging, thereby increasing the demand for health services.

I can't tell you how many times in the last six years I've been asked by health care executives to write a speech based on these three ideas. It's the "Trends in Health Care" speech epidemic. You simply cannot go to a meeting of hospital administrators, insurers, or regulators without hearing *at least* one speaker belabor these three points in excruciating and familiar detail. What amazes me is that the speakers who serve up these hackneyed discoveries actually think they're saying things *nobody* has heard before.

When the topic is tired, rest it. Suggest another. If they won't allow you to change it, then approach it from a unique perspective. And one perspective will always be unique, fresh, and interesting—yours. If you're a beleaguered hospital executive battling the standard, well-known problems, don't waste your time and their good will describing how everyone's having the same problems. Better to talk about what *your* hospital is doing to surmount them. Or, if you think the conventional diagnosis of what ails health care is wrong, offer your own.

RULE 4—*Choose a Topic You Care About*

Groucho Marx once lampooned the speech makers of his day by taking center stage and announcing, "Before I begin my speech, there's something important I want to say." Groucho lived in an age when speech making was a parlor game of overfed plutocrats, each striving to outdo the other with their fatuous puffery. It was also an age when most political speeches were contrived and pompous affairs, transparently devoid of honest conviction. In contrast to— and perhaps in rebellion against—that time when speech making was infested with empty rhetoric and cheap theatrics, today's speakers seem obsessed with dispassion. A "just the facts, ma'am" approach seems the preferred style for all but TV preachers, a few fringe politicians, and a clutch of corporate visionaries.

This development is both good and bad; good because speeches have become more substantial, bad because they've become impersonal. Impersonal speeches tend to be dull, poorly received, and even more poorly remembered.

I think speakers and listeners alike would benefit from more personal speeches. But don't get me wrong. I'm not saying that *all* speeches should bubble and froth. They should not—which is one lesson of the last chapter. And for those who are uncomfortable showing their feelings *at all*, let alone to strangers, a speech is probably not the place to start. Moreover, it's understandably difficult for anyone to work up much of a sweat giving a speech on "New Debt Instruments in the Futures Market."

So when I say you should only give speeches on topics you care about, please don't misunderstand me. I'm not asking you to share your most private thoughts with strangers or that you learn to sob into the microphone. I'm only asking that you give speeches on topics that truly interest you. For two reasons. First, your listeners are more likely to believe what you say if they think *you* believe it. Secondly, you'll enjoy the outing much more if you like your destination.

RULE 5—*Choose a Topic You Can Handle (A Goal You Can Achieve) in the Time Allowed.*

How's this for an ambitious speech title: Thirty Myths about Nicaragua. In all fairness to speaker W. Bruce Weinrod, I don't know the exact circumstances surrounding his more-than-15,000-word speech published in *Vital Speeches of the Day* in May of 1986, just that it was delivered to a law school class in Lexington, Virginia. Assuming he spoke nonstop at a jaunty 150 words per minute, Mr. Weinrod would have wrapped it up in about an hour and forty minutes. However accustomed to auditory punishment, I doubt that any of his listeners could have named more than five of his thirty myths from memory. Mr. Weinrod would have done better had he chosen five of his favorite myths, discussed them in vivid detail, and left the rest to a postspeech handout.

Fidel Castro used to speak for hours at a time. But even

Castro didn't expect anyone to remember what he said. Perhaps he knew that few people can recall more than four major points—no matter how long the speech. Worse yet, beyond twenty minutes, they start to forget those four. This isn't because people are dumb. It's because they're human. So if you're speaking to inform, choose your three to five most important points. Aim to make them stick in twenty minutes or less.

A speech to persuade is another thing altogether. Imagine the difficulty—if not folly—of trying to persuade a chapter of the National Rifle Association to support a total ban on handgun sales. Imagine giving a speech to persuade the board of Planned Parenthood to march in an antiabortion rally. Some things just can't be done in one speech. This doesn't mean they can't be done at all. Maybe a thousand speeches will do the trick. The point is, be realistic—not only about your speaking skills, but also about the attitudes of your listeners.

It is far easier to drag someone one block a day for twelve days than to drag them a mile in one. But if they'll gladly walk at your side, go as far as you can. You may never get another chance.

4

SPEECH
CONSTRUCTION

"God is in the details." This pronouncement of the late
Ludwig Mies van der Rohe still rings down the halls of
architecture. It reminds the builder that paying attention to
the small stuff can make the difference between creating
something of durable beauty and creating something cheap.

Mies van der Rohe's edict is a useful reminder to builders
of speeches as well. If you want to create a masterpiece, you
have to sweat the details. Anyone who's taken the effort to
read this far surely believes this.

But another edict is equally true: "Detail without struc-
ture is vanity." Of what value is a pithy quotation if it makes
an irrelevant point? How persuasive will an argument be if
the steps are out of order? How funny will the joke be if
the punch line comes before the setup? Good speech construction, like any kind of construction, depends on selecting the right materials and arranging them in the proper
order.

But there the analogy between the builder of buildings
and the builder of speeches breaks down. Why? Because
the speech must make sense to the observer *at all times*

during the making. Not so for the building under construction. It is unimportant to the architect and construction boss if onlookers scratch their heads for weeks before understanding the point of all the banging and yelling beyond the barricades. Speech audiences are not so patient.

For this reason building a speech is *unlike* building any other thing because a speech is not a *thing* at all. Unlike things—from novels to navels—a speech cannot be inspected later. Not unless it's published. And really, how many of your speeches will be published, let alone read if they are published? When your speech is finished, it's over. Done, gone, no longer. Your speech must achieve its purpose and have its full effect *during* its delivery. If the job's not done by the time you leave the stage, the speech was a failure.

Because your speech must make sense to your observers as you build, the *order* in which things are done is paramount—absolutely critical to their understanding and your success. The audience needn't grasp the *full significance* of your speech until the end—but they should never be confused about what you're doing at the time.

A speech is not a thing. It's an event.

When you plan a speech, you resemble a composer planning a performance. The performance must be plotted to educate, inspire, or entertain during the execution. The order of presentation matters almost as much as the elements presented. As for these elements, the musician knows many tunes. But which ones should be played? In what order should they be played for maximum effect? What about special effects?

This chapter concerns scripting a speech performance from start to finish—from the opening greeting, through the presentation of material, and on to the exit bow.

THE OPENING

Early in your speech—as early as the first few seconds—
each listener in your audience asks and answers three questions:

- Does the speaker care about me and my situation?
- Is the speaker credible?
- Does the speaker have something to say worth listening to?

Yes answers get you a fair hearing. If the answers are no,
it's unlikely that you'll regain your listener's willing attention during the remainder of the speech, no matter what
you do or say. Doing a good job in the first minute won't
ensure victory. But you can bet that a bad start will promote
an early and ignominious defeat. Consequently, it's well
worth committing to memory a few of the most common
gaffes which are *guaranteed* to turn an audience against you
from the start.

Never Do These Things

- Never tell a racist, sexist, or off-color joke.
- Never tell your listeners you'd rather be somewhere else.
- Never misstate the name of the sponsoring organization.
- Never give a speech while intoxicated or drugged. People
  can tell, and are usually offended.
- Never say you've given the same speech before or that some-
  one else wrote it for you.
- Never intentionally embarrass an audience member in any
  way.

Nobody's perfect. And nobody expects you to be perfect;
just civilized. People in audiences are notoriously sensitive.
Why? Because they've willingly subjected themselves to the

unknown based on the expectation that it will be a good (or at least, tolerable) experience. If that expectation is violated, they'll get nervous, anxious, and perhaps a bit frightened. This is particularly true if something unexpected is demanded of them, like having to somehow participate in the presentation.

Listeners expect an initial display of respect, kindness, and caring from outsiders and superiors alike. Until the speaker passes muster, he or she remains a potential threat. That said, let me quickly encourage you to try your best not to become preoccupied with being judged. Instead, concentrate on doing what you feel is right. If you avoid the big blunders, people will immediately give you the benefit of the doubt. If you show your listeners respect and appreciation, chances are excellent that they'll return the courtesy. Everyone knows how much work goes into a speech.

Five Ways to Start a Speech

Good speech openings last roughly thirty seconds to a minute and a half. Your opening should do four things.

1. Get the listener's attention.
2. Establish your credentials and caring.
3. Give your listener a reason for attending to the remainder of your speech.
4. Smoothly introduce your topic or main idea.

One or all of the following five techniques can be used to accomplish these objectives.

1. *Refer Directly to the Subject of Your Talk*

My fellow citizens, I'd like to speak to you tonight about our future. About a great and historic effort to give the words *freedom, fairness,* and *hope* new meaning and power for every man and woman in America. Specifically, I want to talk about taxes . . . about what we must do as a nation this year to transform a system that's become an endless source of confusion and resentment into one that is clear, simple, and fair for all. . . . A tax code that no longer runs roughshod over mainstreet America.

> —PRESIDENT RONALD REAGAN, *televised address to the nation,*
> *May 1985.*

Reagan's address had been heavily advertised by the three television networks, as well as by newspapers and radio stations across the country. People knew he would be speaking on tax reform—a pocketbook issue of interest to nearly every citizen. His credibility (or at least his authority) established by the office of the presidency, his audience already secured by a news announcer, Reagan began his speech by immediately referring to his subject.

2. *Begin with a Story or Illustration*

When I wrote my Speak Out letter to President Reagan, I congratulated him on having recently celebrated his seventy-fourth birthday. And I told him that I remembered, some three decades ago, wondering if I would be around to celebrate my twenty-fourth.

I very nearly wasn't, and I'd like to tell you a little bit about that.

If I can, I'll begin by saying that I've been married thirty-eight years. I'm the mother of five beloved children, two born prior to the abortion I had, three born after it; the grandma of the three most beautiful babies in the world; and the victim of a rapist and an illegal abortionist.

On my way home from work one night in the mid-1950s. . . .

> —A WOMAN NAMED SHERRY *[last name omitted by request] of*
> *Peoria, IL, speaking for the National Abortion Rights Action*
> *League in the summer of 1985.*

Stories command attention. The best ones are true, personal, and directly related to the point of the speech. Sherry's story is honest, compelling, and leads the audience directly into her speech about the negative consequences of outlawing abortion.

3. *Establish a Common Bond with the Audience*

Ladies and gentlemen: May I say that Oslo, in my personal estimation, is one of the five most beautiful and interesting cities in the world, ranking right up there with Copenhagen, Stockholm, Helsinki, and Araskoga.

Now, surely, all of you have heard of Araskoga. Sweden has it on its map, a crossroads village, if a village can be a dairy, a house, and a church.

In 1978 my then teenage son and I found Araskoga on a mission to locate our forebears in Sweden. We left our car at the crossroads and walked up to the large house across from the Araskoga dairy, rang the doorbell and were met by a querulous Swede. It seems another Araskog had been there not long before, because, when I showed him my card, he looked at the name and wearily sighed, "Oh no, not another one of you. Don't you Americans have anything else to do but look for your ancestors?"

Well, my son looked as if he wondered about the wisdom of our entire expedition, but that encounter was just the beginning. . . . [Araskog then recounts extensive efforts to locate the gravesites of his ancestors.]

As you must have determined by now, I'm proud of being of Scandinavian origin.

> —RAND ARASKOG, *Chairman of International Telephone and Telegraph Corp., speaking to the Norwegian Society of Industrial Engineering and Management, Oslo, Norway, October 7, 1981.* [13]

"I'm one of you." That is the message of this opening, a clear example of the common-bond technique. Connecting with the life and times of the listener is one of the surest ways to gain attention and establish empathy. (But being half-Norwegian myself, I can assure Mr. Araskog that there are better ways to win over a Norwegian than telling him your ancestors were Swedes! And vice versa.)

The common-bond technique is easily trivialized by appeals to meaningless commonalities. A speaker can't get much mileage out of the statement, "It's good to be back in Chicago. My third cousin on my sister's side used to mail-order his knockwurst from a little deli just north of here." Still, even an essentially vacuous reference tells the listener you're trying.

4. *Pay Them an Honest Compliment*

> You know, recently I had three bouts with death. And they told me, "Buscaglia, this is it." I said, "No it isn't." And here I am. I have things to do. . . . Well, for goodness sakes, I had never seen Charlotte [North Carolina] before. You can't die and not see Charlotte!
>
> —LEO BUSCAGLIA, *author and lecturer, speaking in Charlotte, North Carolina, 1985.*

Buscaglia here pays the people of Charlotte the ultimate compliment on their taste in cities—life is not complete until one has seen theirs! Complimenting your listeners on a point of pride says that you care enough to know why it makes them proud. It says you understand their *values*, which is considerably more than saying you've noticed, say, their new topcoat. But compliments of any kind work only if they are deserved and sincerely given. Buscaglia's worked because Charlotte is indeed a beautiful city and it was undeniable from his voice and bearing that Buscaglia was sincere.

5. *Use Humor That Steers Your Audience to the Subject*

There's a cartoon that hangs in the New York offices of "Nightline" showing a beaver and a rabbit in front of a hydroelectric dam. And the beaver is saying, "I didn't exactly build it, but it's based on an idea of mine."

That is true in the particular of "The Crisis Game" which was built by two of my dear friends and colleagues who are here tonight—Bill Lord and Bill Moore—but it is even more true of "Nightline" in general. Television is quite clearly a medium in which nobody does anything by himself. I am enormously grateful to the very talented . . . and for the most part very young . . . staff of "Nightline." It is their work. They are the ones who have constructed the dam.

But I will hold this [award] for them until they get to be old enough to appreciate it.

—TED KOPPEL, *journalist, accepting an award from Columbia University honoring "Nightline," the TV news-interview show.*

A humorous lead of this quality will always please. The key considerations: Is the humor in good taste? Is it fresh? Is it relevant to the main point, that is, will it slide the listener comfortably into the body of the speech?

Jokes and other bits of comic contrivance have long been favored devices for speech openings. Lately, the self-deprecating comment or anecdote is enjoying a burst of popularity. This is where the speaker takes a poke at himself to show he doesn't regard himself as more important than his listeners. For example:

As you know from the introduction, my profession is to write jokes, but my real love is to stand up here and talk about that, and it's kind of predictable that I would go into this profession because extemporaneous speaking kind of runs in my family. Let me give you a little example of what I mean by that. A few years ago, my daughter, who was in kindergarten, came to me and said, "Daddy, I have to recite a poem in school. Would you help me with it?" And I said, "Sure, Honey, but you know Daddy writes for some pretty famous people, so why don't you let me write something for you. Then when you give it at school, it will be funny, it will be different, and it will be completely yours." She thought about that for a while, then she said, "Well, Dad, this is in front of the whole school. I'd rather it be good."[14]

> —GENE PERRET, *comedy writer, in a speech given to the Town Hall of California, Los Angeles, June 11, 1985.*

You may know that Gene Perret is a professional gag writer and humorist. His credits include many hit TV shows as well as work for such people as Bob Hope, Bill Cosby, and Carol Burnett. These credits were announced to his audience during his introduction. So Perret knows his audience expects him to be funny. This he can do. But he wants to do more. He wants to show that humor abounds in our daily affairs. Perret also wants to show that you don't have to be a comedian to have something funny to say. So he makes himself the butt of a piece of humor that illustrates this very point. He tells a warm and simple story about how a small child deflated the self-importance of a grown-up. The generic incident could have occurred in any house mixing adults with children.

Self-deprecating humor is fine in its place. And that place is where the audience feels the speaker is "above" them in some important way—a member of a higher social class, an executive much higher on the corporate ladder, or simply a famous person with "star quality." But if you're just plain Harriet who's been around the block, but hardly around Mars, you need all the stature you can get! Imagine the controller of a large company going before the board of directors and starting his quarterly financial report by saying: "You know, I've got to tell you, back when I was flunking out of accounting school I never thought I'd be handling $3 billion of someone else's money. Ha ha."

6. Combinations of Techniques Are Effective

Here's the opening of an award acceptance keynote speech that uses nearly every technique in the book:

> Thank you for those very, very generous words. I assume some of them were about somebody else and I do hope he was

listening. I truly am awed by this honor. Many are the times I have come to this annual dinner over the last quarter-century and sat where you are sitting tonight. These evenings have had a somewhat special meaning for me because my first professional job as an engineer was at the James Forrestal Research Center at Princeton University . . . which was quite a step up from my previous employment waiting tables at Howard Johnson's! You can imagine my chagrin upon learning that university research assistants are paid less than waiters!

Never, however, in my wildest dreams did I expect to find myself standing up here before you. When I say I am in awe, it is not only by the roll call of truly distinguished citizens who have occupied this podium in the past . . . but also by the unswerving sense of purpose the National Security Industrial Association has exhibited through the years in support of our nation's defense.[15]

> —NORMAN R. AUGUSTINE, *chief executive officer, Martin Marietta Corp., accepting the James Forrestal Memorial Award before the National Security Industrial Association, March 17, 1988.*

Humor, reference to common bonds, a short anecdotal story, compliments to the sponsoring organization—they're all here. Augustine continues after this, using quotations and further personal anecdotes, building a bridge into his tribute to American defense workers, a twenty-five-minute speech to stimulate feelings of pride.

Which Opening Technique Is Best?

· *How much time do you have?* Don't tell a two-minute story if you have only a few minutes to communicate a substantial idea.

· *What's the mood of the occasion?* The more motivated your listeners are to hear your ideas on the topic at hand, the more quickly and seriously you should get into your material. Imagine you're a salesperson who's been trying to get into a certain company for months. Finally the purchasing manager agrees to give you ten minutes to tell him how your product can save him money. For heaven's sakes, don't shilly-shally. Tell him what he wants to hear: "I'm not going to waste your time. You asked me here to tell you how the Omnibot can save you money. Let's get started. The Omnibot saves you money in three ways. First, . . ."

In contrast, if you're addressing the Horticultural Society luncheon on proper pruning technique, you're expected to be a bit more leisurely about getting started. The same is true for after-dinner speaking. In these situations you are part of a social gathering.

Whatever your occasion, strive for a pace and tone that says you belong.

· *Has your credibility been established?*   In speeches to inform, persuade, or activate, your credibility is judged early on. You *may* need to describe your experience and background. Don't rely on your introducer to do this for you. He or she can easily prattle on without enhancing your credibility. And sometimes you will get no introduction whatsoever.

The common-bond technique is a good vehicle for getting in your credentials without sounding self-important. For example: "I'm pleased to be here . . . especially to be in the company of so many people who share my love and concern for the ocean environment. I see our friend Louis Bekins out there in the third row. Whenever I see Louis I remember the times we spent together in the Pacific as volunteers for Greenpeace. Our job was to buzz the bows of Japanese whalers in our Zodiacs and generally interfere with harpooning. After weeks of that on the rolling seas, Louis and I still can't look at each other without turning green. So you'll excuse me, Louis, if I take a look at my notes. . . ."

· *What do you do best?*   Some people simply cannot compliment a crowd without projecting discomfort or insincerity. If you are such a person, then by all means, don't begin your speech groping for something nice to say.

If you're a good storyteller, then tell stories when you can—provided they're brief and connected with your material.

If you have a bagful of humorous bits, use them when you can. Just make certain they meet the taste test and lead to your subject without too much contrivance.

If you can't tell a story to save your hide, have no sense of humor, have trouble complimenting people, and feel you have nothing in common with the group (which is unlikely), then thank them for their time and get right into your subject matter.

THE BODY OF THE SPEECH

Your Thesis Statement—The Nub

After the opening warm-up, you must throw the first pitch. If your warm-up has done its job, your listener is brought to the point of subconsciously saying, "Okay. I'm with you. Tell me what's on your mind." Thus the opening of your speech ends and the body begins. At this psychological moment, which is easier to sense than describe, your listeners expect a succinct statement of the *thesis* or main idea of the speech. Give it to them. Get it right out front, early in the speech, and in the clearest language possible. (There are some exceptions to this, as we'll see, but they are rare.) You want people to understand you and be led by your train of thought. But before they can enjoy it, accept it, develop feelings about it or act on it, they have to understand it.

If the speech is one to inform, persuade, or activate, listeners expect to hear statements like, "I'd like to tell you about . . ." or "It is my position that . . ." or "I'm here to support the view that . . ." or "It's time for us to consider what we can do to. . . ."

If the speech is one to stimulate, listeners expect to hear statements like, "When it comes right down to it, I'm here tonight for one purpose. And that's to pay tribute to the many accomplishments of . . ." or "The death of a friend is a time of sadness and hope. We are sad today that a good woman is gone. Let us remember now why she was our friend . . ." or "Wow! What a first half. First that run-back by number 31. And then Lamson of all people hits Ellis at the fifteen with two seconds remaining—unbelievable!"

If the speech is to entertain, the listener will be suitably notified by comments like, "If I had something important to say, believe me, I'd have said it by now so let's just talk about politics" or "Isn't it wonderful when people know you but don't scream and run away? I owe it all to my charisma course, which I'd like to tell you about now" or "Alice Roosevelt Longworth said it best—'I have a simple philosophy of life. Fill what's empty. Empty what's full. And scratch where it itches.' Well, Alice, we've finished the filling and emptying. How about we get right to the scratching."

Notice that the *thesis statement* does three things.

1. It tells your audience what *kind* of a speech to expect—an informational speech, a persuasive speech, a humorous speech.

2. It sets the tone of your presentation—matter-of-fact, enthusiastic, light-hearted, somber.

3. It contains a hint, a seed, a suggestion, or even a direct statement of how the speaker intends to proceed.

Your Main Ideas

A good speech is based on just a few main ideas. There are many ways to understand how this works. Here are three:

The Speech as a Musical Concert

The speechmaker is like the performing musician. The main selections are chosen, an order of presentation is decided upon, and the selections are played in that order, along with some verbal commentary between them. The musician's selections are the speaker's ideas.

. . . as a "Train of Thought"

Sharon Anthony Bower of Stanford University suggests viewing a speech as a "Train of Thought." The speaker's train consists of *(a)* the opening "engine," complete with attention-getting lights and bells; *(b)* "boxcars" filled with main ideas and supporting points; *(c)* transition statement "car couplers"; and *(d)* a concluding "caboose." The speaker drives the Train of Thought past the listener.[16]

. . . as a Stream of Ideas

Imagine you're standing on a river bank. Your audience is downstream, out of sight. Each of you spend the day watching the river and all that's in it go by. To communicate with the person downstream, you launch small barges, each carrying a billboard. On each billboard you can write only a few words, words that can be easily seen from shore. The river runs quickly, so your audience doesn't have much time to read. You can float up to six billboards to tell them why the river's polluted. You get three to congratulate them on their wedding. You get two billboards to tell them about the break in the dam. You get one billboard to sell them a boat. Besides the swiftness of the river, your biggest problem in communication is the vast number of message barges already in the river. Your challenge: making *your* billboards compelling.

As these three analogies suggest, the speaker's first challenge is always the same—deciding on a pattern of presentation that will display the main ideas not only logically, but memorably. The next section lists some of the many such patterns available. Afterwards, we'll move on to the next element of speech composition—producing the requisite support, elaboration, and emphasis for the ideas themselves.

Organizing Your Main Ideas

The Speech to Inform

Option 1—Formats to Fit the Mind's Filing System

In a piece of thinking that revolutionized Western philosophy, the eighteenth-century German philosopher Immanuel Kant proposed that the human mind isn't a passive recipient of data, but rather a gatekeeper—it allows only certain kinds of information into consciousness. Specifically, Kant said that the mind screens data through three filters: Time, Space, and Cause/Effect. Well, twentieth-century psychologists say Kant was right, at least to this extent: Information that comes to us preorganized according to *when* things happen (time), *where* things happen (space), or *how* things happen (cause/effect) is much easier to understand and remember than information that is not organized at all. And, as we know, information that is understandable and memorable is also more credible than information which is neither. Some examples follow of how speakers can use Kant's great gift.[17]

ORGANIZING BY TIME

Divide your subject into three parts: past, present, and future. For example, suppose your speech is to inform your audience about consumer protection in America. Start by describing the origin of consumer protection laws and agencies, move on to describe what's happening today, and close with a forecast of future issues.

ORGANIZING IN SPACE

Here, your topic is discussed from the point of view of different places. To illustrate, suppose you're the marketing manager of a shoelace company. Your job is to tell senior management how your new colored laces are selling. You break it down by sales regions. "In the Northern states, pastels are moving well, but fluorescents have a ways to go. Down South, we can't keep the argyles on the shelf. Back East, forget it. Sales are off 15 percent. However, in the Western region they're going gaga over polka dots."

ORGANIZING BY CAUSE AND EFFECT

The cause/effect format is useful when the speaker's goal is to explain *why* something is so or otherwise give perspective to an issue. For example, a public official responds to citizens concerned about a recent increase in the crime rate. The first part of her speech is about the *causes* of the increase (new gangs in the city, poverty, poorly functioning court system). The second part of her speech describes the *effects* of the crime wave (numbers of people injured, property losses, increases in insurance rates). This format is particularly useful to the speaker who wants to prepare the audience to consider, and then accept, a specific proposal for improvement—a proposal which attacks the causes as described.

Option 2—Divide Your Topic into
Logical Parts

Unfortunately, speeches often resist organization by time, space, or cause/effect. This is particularly true for abstract topics like Principles of Personal Power or How to Reduce the Federal Deficit. Consider dividing such topics into two to five logical parts.

From the speaker's point of view, each part chosen should be critical to an understanding of the main topic. For example, a lawyer with the Washington State Attorney General's office once gave a speech on the role of his work unit, the Fair Practices Division. He called his speech The Four "Eights": Educate, Investigate, Litigate, Legislate. The organization is memorable because the play on word sounds unifies the four functions (logical parts) of his agency.

Another example: The head of a large hospital was asked to give a speech on "Marketing the Nursing Profession." She broke the topic down into the classical subparts of marketing—product, price, place, promotion. She then discussed how well the profession was being "sold," from the perspective of each of the four—in other words, are nursing services available in the right places? For the right price? And so forth.

If there is any general rule about logical parts presentation it is this: Put your most important point first and your next most important point last. In any list of things, people tend to remember the first and the last. Psychologists call this the "primacy and recency effect."

Option 3—The Extended Metaphor

A speechwriter was asked in early 1981 to draft a speech explaining the four parts of newly elected Ronald Reagan's economic plan. The finished speech said Reagan saw the needs of the economy to be similar to those of a hiker lost in the desert, the victim of an outdated map and a faulty compass. To make matters worse, the hiker was out of water. The hiker needed a new map to follow, so did the economy—one showing landmarks of reduced spending and business deregulation. The hiker needed a reliable compass, so did the economy—one pointing the way toward restraint in the growth of the money supply. Finally, the hiker needed a quick injection of energy, and so did the economy—tax cuts to increase investments in productive enterprises.

Another example: A businessman wanted to explain to his employees why they would embark on a new business strategy, a strategy designed to maintain revenues despite increased competition. He compared his organization to a bee hive sitting in a field of flowers and trees. For years, he said, theirs was the only hive in the field. But recently, a truck had come through and placed several new hives around the area (new competition). The rest of the speech described what the bees from the old hive would have to do to survive. The key to the bees' survival paralleled the new business strategy—cultivate the most productive accounts (stick with them and help them produce more), and leave the marginal producers to the competition.

The extended metaphor technique is powerful because it lets the speaker communicate a large body of information without having to explain all the details. If the metaphor is apt, the listener fills in the details automatically. Secondly, metaphors add clarity and credibility to abstract ideas by linking them with everyday events and natural processes. Third, extended metaphors are useful because they hold attention.

The only danger is appearing whimsical if the wrong metaphor is chosen. But sometimes this is a small price to pay for achieving the goal of comprehension.

Which Pattern of Organization Is Best?

Remember your audience and the occasion. If the audience is restless, the time short, and the topic urgent, follow Winston Churchill's advice: "If you have an important point to make, don't be subtle or clever. Use a pile driver."

Subtle forms of organization, like the extended metaphor, work best with well-rested, unhurried, highly interested listeners who not only can tolerate, but actually enjoy some ambiguity.

Organization based on time, space, and cause/effect works well with all listeners, but especially with those who are highly visual and tactile—people who work with their hands, who enjoy travel, who work in the performing arts, or labor in any profession that requires constant attention to how things, people, and places are organized in time and space.

The logical parts format works well with managers, attorneys, executives, and technical experts who spend their days analyzing data and solving problems. These professions require the ability to break complex problems into component parts, a skill which matches the methodology of the logical parts format.

The Speech to Persuade

Option 1—Problem/Solution

The speaker first describes a problem, then presents a solution. This is a time-honored (and timeworn) strategy. Its virtue lies in simplicity, its sin in overuse.

Option 2—Monroe's Motivated Sequence

This technique is named after its inventor, Alan H. Monroe, a former professor of communication at Purdue University, who died in 1975.

Using Monroe's formula, the speaker works through a predetermined sequence of steps designed to motivate the listener to take the suggested action. Technically, this format is for speeches intended to activate. But if the speaker concludes after the fourth step, it also works fine as a persuasive model. The steps:

Attention.   Simply that, get their attention. Normally recommended by Monroe disciples is an opening story that shows something is terribly wrong.

Need.   In this step, the speaker shows that the problem illustrated by the opening example is commonplace, that, *in general,* improvement is needed.

Satisfaction.   The speaker describes his or her proposal, the solution that will eliminate the problem and answer the need.

Visualization and Contrast.   A critical step where the speaker paints a verbal picture of the world as it will be when the problems first discussed are gone, replaced by a better state of affairs brought about by the satisfaction step.

Action.   This step goes beyond persuasion. It is where the speaker implores the audience to take *action* to bring about the solution proposed in the satisfaction step.[18]

Option 3—Indirect Proof

This method is prescribed when the audience is predisposed to reject the speaker's main point regardless of the evidence he or she might have.

For example, a speaker wanting to convince the California Vegetable Growers' Association to support tougher immigration laws would probably get nowhere starting off by saying "We need tougher immigration laws and I want to tell you why." Another approach is needed.

The strategy of indirect proof is to avoid stiffening resistance by convincing the audience of the supporting evidence *before* announcing the thesis. For example, "I want to talk to you about a problem that's against everything we believe in as a compassionate, even-handed people. You may not be aware of what's happening, but I assure you, it is within your power to stop it. Most people I know are surprised and shocked to learn that thirty people are found murdered each month in our county because of this . . . that's one a day . . . many of them children . . . dead in the trunks of cars . . . stuffed in dumpsters . . . or dehydrated and left for dead at the side of the road. You might also be surprised to learn that . . ."

After a few minutes of this, the speaker reveals what some may already have guessed: the speech is about the high human cost of the illegal use of immigrant labor. The speaker's case sounds more convincing when the listeners are not given early warning to set up their defensive rationalizations.

Option 4—Answering the Objections

This approach is used (1) when the position advocated by the speaker is known by the audience, (2) where significant objections to it have previously reached their ears, and (3) where the audience will likely hear more objections later.

The steps are simple. The speaker first thanks the audience for the opportunity to speak and state his case. A compliment is usually paid to the audience next for keeping an open mind on the issue. (Even if their minds are closed, saying they remain open will indeed open them a crack—nobody likes to admit they don't have an open mind!) After this, the speaker states his position, clearly states the *main* objections to it, and then attempts to refute these objections with the best evidence available. And so on down through the weakest objection. At the end, the speaker will be refut-

ing the opposition's weakest arguments, so the audience
will be likely to remember the opposing position as being
supported by weak arguments.

To be effective, the speaker must not set up a straw man
to knock down, but instead attempt to refute the best of the
opposing arguments in addition to the weakest.

Option 5—Humor and Satire

Every so often, a speaker will sense that a rational approach will not work. Instead, the speaker resorts to poking
light-hearted fun at the opposing view or unleashing unbridled satire. The best examples of satire today are not in
speeches, but in the newspaper columns of Art Buchwald,
Mike Royko, Henry Gay, Dave Barry, and Russell Baker.
Just about the only full-time, on-stage satirist these days is
Mark Russell. Will Rogers was one of the country's greatest
speakers, using light-hearted humor as well as biting satire
as his preferred methods of argument.

It takes not just great intelligence and a keen wit to pull
off a humorous persuasive speech, but also significant acting
talent.

Option 6—Reframing the Issue

Options 1 through 5 all depict the persuasive process as
essentially combative—the speaker has an idea and tries to
prove it superior to an opposing view already in circulation.
Reframing the issue means not trying to show that one
position is right and another is wrong. Instead, the speaker
works to show that people would be more able to achieve
their goals if they look at the issue in another way.

A good example of reframing the issue took place during the 1988 Summer Olympic Games in South Korea. A
handful of athletes were barred from competition or

stripped of their medals because tests showed they had used illegal drugs during training; anabolic steroids were the usual find.

Savvy sports officials did not say these drugs should be prohibited because users have an unfair advantage over nonusers and that's not sporting or fair. Instead, they argued that athletes will perform *better* over time if they refrain from steroid use—that steroids are dangerous substances, shortening the careers, and sometimes the lives, of competitive athletes.

Which approach is more likely to keep young athletes off steroids? Telling them the drugs will give them an unfair advantage? Or giving them evidence that they'll perform better if they stay away from them? The latter, because it directly addresses what leads people to steroids in the first place—the desire to be a superior athlete.

The reframing technique is best used to overcome great resistance and to shape the debate before it begins. Salespeople and politicians employ this method relentlessly. We'll take another look at this in chapter 10.

The Speech to Activate

As illustrated in Monroe's Motivated Sequence (above), the speech to activate is a speech to persuade with one step added at the end—the directive. For example: When the minister has persuaded his flock that a church in financial ruin would be a misery for all, he tells them exactly how they can keep such a thing from happening. This is the action step. "Brethren, your soul may survive on faith alone, but your church cannot. I ask you now to reach into your wallet as well as your heart. When the collection plate comes to you, add what you can to the offering of your neighbors. Remember, your prosperity comes from God. Show Him that you're grateful for His bounty. Place some of that money in His hand . . . in the plate that symbolizes His setting at your table."

Whether you're asking someone to buy your goods or sign your petition, once you've persuaded them, you must tell them *exactly* what it is you want them to do. The directions must be clear, easy to follow, and immediate. The longer the interval between the peak persuasive moment and the time they are supposed to act, the less likely they will be to act.

The Speech to Stimulate

Speeches to stimulate can be organized just like speeches to inform. For example, a speaker at a political rally will commonly whip up loyalty to the candidate by breaking the job down into two logical parts: (1) reasons why their candidate is so wonderful and (2) reasons why the opponent is so terrible. The pep talk to the football team at halftime can be organized around what happened on different parts of the playing field (space), during different quarters (time), or within different plays (cause/effect).

The Speech to Entertain

The most important thing to remember about organizing speeches to entertain is this: It doesn't matter *how* they are organized, so long as they *are*. What separates a stand-up comedy routine from a speech to entertain is a theme. A theme gives a purpose to the many individual bits of humor that illustrate it. For example, a humorous graduation speech might be built around the idea that whenever people begin on difficult journeys, others rush forward to give them worthless but well-meant advice. The speech would consist of humorous examples throughout the ages—some true, some not. What would make the speech rise above all the individual bits is that together they illustrate a meaningful point about humanity—that people are an endearing mixture of empathy and egocentricity.

Supporting Your Ideas

Sometimes we don't need to give reasons for what we say. That *we* said it is enough. "Help, my house is on fire." That one sentence, spoken with conviction from the front door, will activate legions under most circumstances. Nobody asks us *how* we know our house is on fire. If we don't know, who does? And if you're telling people when the next meeting of the club will be, and you are the club president, nobody would be foolish enough to say, "How do you know that?" You do because *you* schedule the meetings.

When it *is* necessary to support our ideas, that support is usually one of two kinds: reasons and elaboration. We give reasons when we are trying to prove or establish something, or justify our belief in something. Other times, giving support means *elaborating* on our ideas to make them clearer, or more stimulating or more entertaining.

Various Kinds of Support for Your Ideas

Whether you want to clarify, embellish, or argue for your ideas, you need material. The following kinds of supporting material are most common:

Facts

Rushing River National Park is overcrowded. Today, there's only thirty square feet of park space for every visitor, whereas in 1950 there was three hundred square feet. It is ten times more crowded today than in 1950.

To gain the most advantage from facts and statistics, remember first what Lord Nelson said upon defeating Napoleon at Trafalgar: "Only numbers annihilate." His comment is as true for numbers in speeches as it is for numbers in battle. Numbers should be used sparingly in speeches.

Moreover, whenever statistics are used, they should be stated in a way that helps the listener grasp their significance. It's wise to translate all statistical support into terms familiar to your listener.

Before:

1988 inflation in Nicaragua has been 10,000 percent.

After:

If America had inflation at the same rate as Nicaragua this past year, this pineapple that costs fifty cents would instead cost fifty dollars.

—GARRICK UTLEY, *NBC News, Managua, Nicaragua, 11/88.*

Before:

33 percent of the average worker's pay goes for FICA, sales, and income tax.

After:

If you start work at nine in the morning and quit at five, you work for your government 'til about noon.

Before:

10 percent of all girls get pregnant before they leave high school.

After:

Go into any high school cafeteria at lunchtime and ask every tenth girl to stand. Do that in every high school in the country.

That'll give you a rough idea of how many girls will either have a baby or an abortion before they can legally sign a contract or vote.

Before:

Our new headquarters building has a computer center that occupies 40 percent of the building—over 380,000 square feet of floor space.

After:

Let's compare the size of our headquarters building with the average home of 2,000 square feet. The computer center alone would fill every room of 190 such homes. And the computer center takes up less than half the building.

Before:

There's a 60 percent wholesale discount on this item.

After:

When you buy ten of these at our discount price, you have to sell only four to break even. The rest are profit.

To use statistics well, you must clarify their significance. Otherwise they're just numbers.

Illustrations

Rushing River National Park is overcrowded. Last year, John and Mary Urban and their two children climbed in the family car to revisit the Rushing River National Park that John and Mary had known as children. They never found it. When they arrived at the six-lane park entrance after an eight-hour drive, they waited behind a half mile of cars just to get past the registration booth. Once inside the park boundary, what they found was worse. . . .

An illustration is usually a verbal portrait of your idea.
Illustrations do not prove anything. John and Mary may just
have hit the park on a bad day. Illustrations clarify the
meaning of your ideas, helping your listeners understand
your point of view.

Illustrations can also classify abstract ideas. For example,
a speaker wishing to illustrate the point that only results
lead to fame might quote Henry Ford's comment, "You
can't build a reputation on what you're *going* to do." This
is not proof, only enhancement.

Examples

Rushing River National Park is overcrowded. Take Rainbow
Arch campground as an example. When this lovely spot by
the river was developed into campsites, it was planned for a
maximum of twenty-five campers a night. Last season, the
daily population of Rainbow Arch campground was four
times that—one hundred a night; the people outnumbered
the trees.

Examples clarify, but they do more. Examples are a kind
of evidence. They document the speaker's claim. While one
example usually does not prove a claim, a single example
can often be used to disprove one. For instance, all one has
to do to disprove the notion that poor people are poor
because they are lazy is to point to one hardworking poor
person. This is called a *counterexample*.

Expert Testimony

Rushing River National Park is overcrowded. Head Ranger
Harvey Hemlock told me yesterday that he felt more like a
cruise-ship director than a forest ranger.

Testimony is only as effective as the source is credible to the listener. For example, by most accounts President Jimmy Carter lost considerable stature in a 1980 televised debate against Republican challenger Ronald Reagan. To support his claim that nuclear disarmament was a top-priority foreign policy objective, President Carter referred to a conversation he had with his daughter Amy, then nine years old. The press and the Republicans savaged Carter for relying on children to guide American foreign policy. In retrospect, we know that President Carter quoted Amy to remind us that our children's future is our first responsibility. But in a highly contentious and polarized debate, with Carter slipping in the polls, this was a perfect opening for those who thought Carter was "weak on defense."

Metaphor

Rushing River National Park is overcrowded. Visitors are as thick as fur on a squirrel, but not nearly as laid-back.

The chief purpose of metaphor is to make vague ideas concrete by associating them with vivid images.

Analogy

Rushing River National Park is overcrowded. Have you ever seen what happens when too many rats are put in a box? First, they become more aggressive in staking out and defending their territory. Does this remind anyone of the tent-pitching frenzy that consumes Rainbow Arch campground on Friday nights?

Analogies are not admissible evidence in a court of law. But they are powerful persuaders. We'll take frequent note of analogies in the chapters ahead.

Various Kinds of Claims

By using many kinds of supporting material, you'll add clarity and credibility to your ideas. Another aspect of providing good support for ideas is matching the kind of support used with the kind of claim advanced.

When a speaker makes a claim, it is usually one of three kinds: a claim of fact, a claim of policy, or a claim of value. Supporting material *should vary* with the kind of claim being made.

Claims of Fact

The ozone layer in our atmosphere is being destroyed by fluorocarbon gas.

It is more economical to renovate the old fire station than to build a new one.

The principal force behind the influx of illegal workers in California is poverty in Latin America.

Factual claims are supported by other facts. Take the claim about the ozone layer. To support it, the speaker would need evidence that the ozone layer was more dense before fluorocarbons were widely used; that fluorocarbons do, in fact, break down ozone gas; that all other likely explanations for the ozone erosion had been scientifically rejected; and so on. This evidence could, for example, come in the form of expert testimony from atmospheric scientists or statistics from research studies.

Claims of Policy

Airline manufacturers should be required to recall and repair defective aircraft.

Sea otters should be put on the list of protected species.

Management should approve the proposal for on-site day care.

Claims of policy are supported by facts *within the context of other policies.* In the case of the sea otters, the speaker must show not only that sea otters are in danger of extinction, *but also* that it is or has been the policy of the government to protect any and all species which are in danger of extinction. Appeals to precedent, law, or procedures are needed to support claims of policy.

Claims of Value

It is wrong to discriminate on the basis of sexual preference.

Everyone convicted of first-degree murder should be put to death.

All South Africans should have an equal voice in the government of South Africa.

Claims of value are ethical or moral statements. They are supported best by showing how they follow directly from moral standards already held by the audience. For example, the claim that all South Africans should have the right to vote is often supported by the argument that universal suffrage and one-man–one-vote rule is a natural right, not one that can be given or taken away by government.

Transition Statements

We've seen that the body of a good speech consists of a few main ideas clearly argued and well elaborated. It is also organized in a way helpful to the speaker's purpose. There's one element remaining—transition statements to bridge the main points.

Use them. Use them. Use them. Simple comments to tell the listener where you are, where you've been, and where you're going should be sprinkled liberally throughout your material.

> That's the first reason why I believe we should. . . . But there's another reason. And it's this. . . .

> You see, my experience with this kind of work is strong. . . .

> So when you think of Acme, you'll think *durability*. But you'll also think *efficiency*. Here's why. According to a recent survey. . . ."

THE CLOSING

Four Quick Rules

RULE 1.—*End on time.*

St. Ambrose, the fourth-century bishop of Milan, said "A speech that is wearisome only stirs up anger." What St. Ambrose said fifteen hundred years ago is true today. Just ask Governor Bill Clinton of Arkansas. Clinton had the job of introducing the 1988 Democratic presidential nominee, Michael Dukakis, at the Democratic National Convention. Clinton spoke so long over his allotted time that when he finally said, "In conclusion," the delegates gave him his only standing ovation.

RULE 2.—*End with conviction.*

A speaker who concludes by saying, "Well, I guess that's all I have to say," may be telling the truth, but will leave the

listener feeling let down and incomplete. Droopy, incon-
clusive endings are common. Speakers are often too sapped
of energy to make a sprint to the finish. And many scrimp
on their endings because they run out of preparation time
the night before while still mired in the body of the speech.

RULE 3.—*End on target.*

Use the last sixty to ninety seconds of a fifteen-minute
speech to emphasize the main ideas of your speech. Never
introduce new material at the end. Digressions into extraneous material only irritate and confuse listeners who want
closure on what has already been said.

RULE 4.—*Tell them you are ending—then do it.*

Listeners expect fair warning when the end of the speech is
near. They expect to hear lines like: "With that as my final
point," or "It's time to bring our discussion to a close," or
"To conclude my report," or "There's no better way to end
than with a story about." After the forewarning, audiences
expect to be carried briskly and directly toward the final
"Thank you."

Five Ways to End a Speech

End with a Brief Story That Illustrates Your Main Point

No one should worry that they can never do enough [to help
others less fortunate]. It is enough to do what you can. I'd like
to close with a brief story that makes this point. The story is
about President Harry Truman and a trip he once made to the
old west town of Tombstone, Arizona.

Now, the streets of Tombstone are crowded with the ghosts of the famous and notorious alike. People like Wyatt Earp and Doc Holliday. But when Truman returned from Tombstone, he didn't talk much about the legendary heros. No. He liked instead to recall the words engraved on the headstone of a simple man buried at Boot Hill. The inscription read: "Here lies Jack Williams. He done all he could."

I thank you . . . *everyone* . . . for doing all *you* can.

> —PERCY ROSS, *philanthropist, in a speech to the Knoxville News-Sentinel 1988 High School Honors Banquet, March 17, 1988.*

End with a Quotation or Ringing Phrase

And finally, my friends, in the staggering task that you have assigned me, I shall always try "to do justly, to love mercy, and to walk humbly with God."

> —ADLAI STEVENSON, *quoting the prophet Micah in his acceptance of the Democratic nomination for president, July 26, 1952.* [19]

Conclude with a Poem

The toll exacted by relentless striving under stress is well stated in a poem by Natasha Josefowitz. I'd like to close my presentation on stress and the organization by reading her perceptive poem in full. It is called, "I Have Arrived."

> I have not seen the plays in town
>   only the computer printouts
> I have not read the latest books
>   only *The Wall Street Journal*
> I have not heard birds sing this year
>   only the ringing of phones
> I have not taken a walk anywhere
>   but from the parking lot to my office
> I have not shared a feeling in years
>   but my thoughts are known to all

> I have not listened to my own needs
>   but what I want I get
> I have not shed a tear in ages
>   I have arrived
> Is *this* where I was going?

—JAN SALISBURY, *psychotherapist and organizational consultant,
in a presentation to the Washington State Attorney General's
State Conference, September 1986.* [20]

End with an Example of Your Theme

The American dream is a song of hope that rings through the
night winter air. . . . We see the dream coming true in the spirit
of discovery of Richard Cavoli [two-line story]. . . . We see the
dream glow in the towering talent of twelve-year-old Tyronne
Ford [two-line story]. . . . We see the dream being saved by
the courage of thirteen-year-old Shelby Butler [two-line story].
. . . And we see the dream born again in the joyful compassion
of thirteen-year-old Trevor Ferrell [two-line story]. . . .

Would you four stand up for a moment? Thank you. You are
the heroes of our hearts. We look at you and know it's true—in
this land of dreams fulfilled where greater dreams may be
imagined, nothing is impossible, no victory is beyond our
reach; no glory will ever be too great.

—PRESIDENT RONALD REAGAN, *State of the Union address,
February 4, 1986.* [21]

Summarize Your Main Ideas

In conclusion, [corporate] restructuring is here to stay. The
data has been analyzed, the results are in, and the restructuring
philosophy has been almost universally adopted. Resisting will
only postpone the cure. It's not a matter of now or never;
restructuring is inevitable in corporate America because it's
economically driven.

It may be painful at times, but we in this country will be
stronger as a result.

—T. BOONE PICKENS, JR., *capitalist, in a speech to the Economic
Club of Detroit, May 2, 1988.* [22]

To End a Speech—Summary

- End your speech on time.
- End your speech with advance notice.
- End your speech to emphasize your main ideas.
- End your speech with conviction.
- End your speech briskly.

5

PERSONAL, CLEAR, AND INTERESTING

Why does the good speech satisfy? If we catalogued favorable comments made by listeners after hearing good speeches, three statements would arise repeatedly: "It was easy to understand," "I felt like he was talking to me," and "It was interesting."

PERSONAL, NOT REMOTE

When I wrote speeches for business executives, I met many who were unwilling to talk about what *they* thought or felt. Instead, they preferred the role of anonymous team member or spokesperson. They were reluctant to use the word *I*.

Like the utterings of Jeeves, P. G. Wodehouse's overbred butler, many of their speeches had a distant, To-whom-it-may-concern feel.

Connecticut National appreciates the opportunity it has been given by the Downtown Development Association to fulfill its corporate mission of engaging in significant and meaningful dialogue with the various civic groups which have been so influential in helping Con National build an effective partnership in the community.

Sadly, many strive daily to disappear into the vast corporate "We." Some merely follow the bad example of their superiors. Others give speeches on remote control because they've been told to. Recruited by the company's speakers' organization and pushed out the door with a script that looks more like a term paper than a speech, loyalty and the lack of time to make revisions conspire against their better judgment.

Granted, in some situations we expect to hear Representative Mouthpiece talk from behind the official seal. Government press aides woodenly read official statements verbatim. On-camera news reporters are expected to sound authoritatively distant. But these are the exceptions.

We normally expect those who talk with us to project signs of personality—to tell us "where they're coming from," in the vernacular of the day. We neither expect nor want florid displays of self-absorption, just personality—a unique self shining through.

If you give a speech that *anyone* could have given, your listeners are likely to conclude that you don't care much about what you're saying.

Speak in the First Person

You speak for yourself, so you might as well sound like it. Regardless of whose payroll you're on, your listeners will assume you speak your own thoughts—that you believe what you say. There's no hiding behind the faceless empire. Notice the difference in tone between these two ways of expressing the same idea:

As facts demand, this officer finds the aforementioned report to be without value.

Jones's report is worthless. I think the facts are clear.

Taking a stand is not egocentric. It is leadership. Talk in the first person.

Edit Out Speech-Talk

Imagine yourself speaking confidently, easily, to a friend you know very well. Do you say, "Dave, turning now to the major issues of the day, let's have lunch"? I hope not! Eliminating stock speech phrases like "I'm honored and delighted to be here before you today" will give you a more conversational tone. And a conversational tone is usually more credible than one straining with artificiality.

Address the Audience as "You"

Instead of this:

Advancement opportunities for new employees of Griswald Imports, such as we have here today at this orientation, are unlimited and tailored to meet individual skills.

Say this:

When you work for Griswald, you choose your own path. Nobody's going to force you onto a treadmill. But I'll guarantee you this—your skills will determine your path and if those skills are good, your path is up.

Don't Mention the Clock

The fragile and happy illusion of a personal conversation between speaker and audience is easily broken. The speaker can shatter this pleasant mirage by loudly noting how much time remains. Saying "In the ten minutes I have left" will cause a flurry of watch checking, effectively distancing the speaker once again.

Their Trust Is Your Currency

Spend it, but don't squander it. A speaker with a good reputation will make any idea more credible simply by saying he believes it. Advertisers in the 1980s, never shy to overwork a good thing, pushed legions of popular chief executives before the cameras to pitch their firms' products—from cars to electric shavers. The principle, called "personal proof," is the idea that a claim backed by the reputation of an apparently honest and sincere person with a history of accomplishment is persuasive.

If you've been doing something well for a good long time, appeal to your own experience every once and a while. Doing so will up the ante for listeners predisposed to reject all they hear. It will also make you sound like you care about what you're saying. For example, "I've been an engineer with this company for twenty-four years. And I have never, never been through a 'surprise' federal safety inspection that I didn't hear about *days* earlier." Personal proof can have the feel of a gambler turning over his last card, and in this case, that's exactly what it is.

CLEAR, NOT CONFUSING

Like a Christmas tree set ablaze by its candles, many a speech has been ruined by its ornamentation.

When your speech *must* excel at transmitting information from you to them, use a clear, strong signal, unadorned by subthemes, nuances, and fluffy windage. The more compli-

cated or controversial your main ideas, the harder you must
fight for clarity. I remember working for a health-care executive who had little success in his campaign to inform the
public of a new idea. This executive worked for what are
today called managed care systems (MCSs). His main idea
was that these MCSs *save the patient money* because they don't
give physicians a financial incentive to overtreat, and thus
overcharge. In contrast, he said, stands the fee-for-service
world of medicine. It is easy to squander money there, he
claimed, because doctor and patient are insulated from cost.
Third-party insurance provides a thick (and deceptively expensive) blanket of price insulation.

Well, this is what he said, but it wasn't what people heard.
Many heard him say, "Managed care systems *make money* by
cutting back on *patient care.*" His speeches were doing as
much harm as good.

It's easy to give people the wrong idea. They search for
it. Sometimes they practically rip it out of your hands. To
avoid giving misunderstanding the advantage, observe the
elements of clarity that follow.

Both comprehension and retention can be increased by
following the same rules. But—and this goes for speech
making in general—following the rules is easier said than
done. And, as we shall soon see, more easily written than
said.

Nine Ways to Improve Clarity

Use Simple Words

"Speech was given to man to conceal his thoughts," huffed
eighteenth-century French statesman Charles-Maurice de
Talleyrand-Périgord after a tedious session with the British.
Or so the story goes. Senator Benjamin Gibbs Macadoo

noticed the same problem when he described a speech given by then-President Rutherford B. Hayes as "an army of pompous phrases moving across the landscape in search of an idea."

Today, many public speakers make the mistake of talking the way they write; they use what author Edwin Newman calls the "boneless and gassy" language of interoffice memos, term papers, and management reports. This language is bad enough in written form. But it is horrid in speeches. It makes the speaker sound stuffy, overreaching in a search for profundity, and certainly more interested in impressing than communicating. Worse yet, the language confuses people. Here's a sample passage of gobbledegook from twentieth-century industrialist Robert C. Galvin, chairman of Motorola, Inc.:

> I foresee an opportunity and a likelihood that the nation which masters the grand management of information for the prime services industries of the service sector in the major developed world markets is destined to global economic leadership of historic proportions.[23]

Say what?

How can we reduce confusion and boost clarity? Here are some examples.

Complex:
I wish to underscore the necessity of adopting a frugal mentality.

Simpler:
I want to stress the need for greater care in spending.

Simpler Yet:
We've got to be more careful about how we spend our money.

Here's a list of simple replacements for complicated words which too often appear in speeches.

Complicated	*Simpler Substitute*
for	because
accomplished	did
respond	answer
utilize	use
persists	continues
conduct	run
sizeable	large
essential	necessary
primary	first
consistent	steady
annually	every year

The simpler expression is not always shorter.

Reduce Jargon

Edwin Newman once gave a speech that I had the good luck to hear. Newman complained marvelously about speeches that "groan with false dignity." He quoted General Alexander Haig, who said, "We must push this to a lower decibel of public fixation." Newman said, "Haig speaks in a code to which no one has the key."

Mr. Newman, like Rudolf Flesch, William Strunk, and E. B. White before him, has been a leader in the clear speech movement.[24] One of the pet peeves of the clear speech movement is jargon.

Some jargon is code—only people in the know understand it, like "We've experienced a negative patient outcome," meaning that the patient died.

Some jargon is shorthand—fewer words to express a mouthful, like FIFO, the accounting principle of first in, first out.

And finally, some jargon is slang: "The car comes complete with fiddle and stove," meaning, to the salesperson, that the car has a radio and heater.

Code and slang are exclusive. When used in speeches, listeners feel talked down to . . . unless they and the speaker are in the know. Then they love it. But being in the know is more than just knowing what the words mean. Few things are more humorous than old people trying to speak like teenagers.

The main thing to remember about verbal shorthand is this: It's as tedious to hear as written shorthand is to read. Yes, it can speed the saying of many things, but as Mohandas Gandhi said, "There's more to life than increasing its speed."

Use More Words per Square Thought

Experts on writing say, "Get rid of as many words as possible." Each word must do something important. If it doesn't, get rid of it. Well, this doesn't work for speaking.

It takes more words to introduce, express, and adequately elaborate an idea in speech than it takes in writing. Why is this so? First, because while the reader can reread, the listener cannot rehear. Speakers do not come equipped with a replay button. Because listeners are easily distracted, they will miss many pieces of what a speaker says. If they miss the crucial sentence, they may never catch up. This makes it necessary for speakers to talk *longer* about their points, using more words on them than would be used to express the same idea in writing.

Second, to emphasize a point in a speech it is not enough to say, "That was my most important point." You must spend *more time* on it than on any other idea. Of several points made in a speech, people tend to remember what speakers talk about *the longest,* especially if the elaboration is unified by a rhetorical technique of the sort explained in chapter 9.

Third, the mind needs adequate processing time to get something into memory. Psychologists call this the "rehearsal effect." It explains why people remember so little of what they hear on the television news—exceedingly brief coverage of individual stories plus too little processing time between them.

Dr. Jerry Tarver notes a good example of an accomplished speaker using what any copy editor would call "redundant" language—an excessive number of words to express a single thought.[25]

> A house divided against itself cannot stand. I believe this government cannot endure permanently half slave and half free. I do not expect the Union to be dissolved . . . but I do expect it will cease to be divided. It will become one thing or the other. Either the opponents of slavery will arrest the further spread of it, and place it where the public mind shall rest in the belief that it is in the course of ultimate extinction; or its advocates will push it forward, till it shall become alike lawful in all the States, old as well as new—North as well as South.
>
> —ABRAHAM LINCOLN

He's no Abe Lincoln, but Lee Iacocca, current chairman of Chrysler Corporation, is one of the most sought-out speakers in America. When Iacocca's finished, people *know* what he talked about. One reason is that he takes *time* to develop his ideas. An example is his elaboration of the idea that a competitive economy depends on the encouragement of risk taking.

> You see, the first thing you have to be able to do to compete is take a risk. If you can't afford to take a risk, then you can't afford to compete. And what we're doing to ourselves in this

country right now is making it more and more difficult to take even a small risk.

If you're a drug company, for example, you don't want to mess around with vaccines. Too risky. A simple vaccine for diphtheria and whooping cough that cost twelve cents a shot in 1980 costs twelve dollars today, and almost all of that cost increase goes into a liability fund.

A small company in Virginia that made driving aids for handicapped people went out of business because it couldn't afford the liability insurance. Too risky.

There used to be eighteen companies making football helmets in this country, but the liability crisis has pared them down to just two. Nobody makes gymnastics equipment or hockey equipment anymore. Too risky.

We've virtually stopped making light aircraft in this country. The biggest production cost is the liability insurance. Too risky.

One of these days we're going to wake up and say, "The hell with it—competing is just too risky."

> —LEE A. IACOCCA, *chairman of the board, Chrysler Corporation, in a speech to the American Bar Association Annual Convention, August 10, 1987.* [26]

Iacocca's second sentence simply rewords his first. Then, instead of giving one or two examples, he clarifies his point with five short ones. And after each example, he *repeats* the key concept—"Too risky." He closes with an exaggeration to drive his point home. He's stated his point well. But most importantly, the listener understands it. That's the difference between stating a point and *really* making one.

Shorten Your Sentences

The ear is smaller than the mouth. Many sentences formed easily by the latter just won't fit in the former. So they stack up outside while comprehension slips away. Listeners need time to absorb ideas. Give it to them. Reduce the volume of information carried by each sentence by making them shorter. And remember to pause often.

Before:

> If the twentieth century has taught us nothing else it should at least have taught us that while war undoubtedly creates refugees, the peace that follows upon the victory of totalitarian political forces will create even more refugees and greater inhumanities than those that accompany war itself.
>
> —ALAN NELSON, *commissioner, U.S. Immigration and Naturalization Service.* [27]

After:

> War creates refugees. This lesson of the twentieth century is clear. But another lesson should be equally clear. When totalitarian forces win, the peace that follows creates more refugees than the war itself. And the inhumanities of the so-called peace will exceed the inhumanities of war.

Speak from Known to Unknown

Explain new ideas by reference to things and ideas already familiar to the listener. Not this:

> This new machine produces eighty copies per minute.

But this:

> Remember that copier you bought last year? This one's twice as fast.

Analogies and metaphors work exceptionally well in introducing new ideas. Theodore H. White, Pulitzer Prize–winning expert on American politics, illustrated the clarifying power of analogies when he responded to the question, "What effect has television had on politicians?" White answered, "Politicians remind me of a certain variety of plant—the kind that grow under porches and other places where the sun doesn't penetrate. Botanists call these plants *heliotropic,* meaning that as they grow, they bend in the direction of the sun. Well, politicians today are what I call *Videotropic.* As they grow, they follow the camera because that's where the votes are." White's metaphor started with something everyone's seen—a plant curving toward the sun. Then he put a label on that concept—*Heliotropic.* He then defined *heliotropic* because it was the setup for the "videotropic" punch line. Each step rested on the foundation laid before.[28]

Present Only a Small Number of Main Ideas

When you realize how long it takes to verbally introduce, state, elaborate on, and support an idea, you begin to realize there's never enough time to communicate all you'd like. One to five main ideas is about all your audience will ever give you the time and attention to deliver. It follows that the more complex and unfamiliar your material, the more skillful—artful—you must be in presentation.

Use Transition Statements

Tell your audience where you've just been and where you're going next. Transition statements are anchors for drifting attention.

Excessive Detail Obscures Clarity

Novice technical speakers tend to burden the listener with detail. Speaking about our jobs and hobbies, it's easy to get carried away. There's a point at which adding detail no longer improves comprehension, but produces confusion instead.

Keep Moving Forward

Clarity depends on purpose and clear movement toward the goal. As long as there is purpose and motion, the pace can vary, and should. Good speeches can flow like summer streams on the Irish countryside. Or they can rush ahead like swollen mountain rivers, covering ground swiftly and sweeping away all in their path. But rarely will a good speech move frenetically like a mad hornet in a fruit jar. In the good speech, all movement is forward, with some resting to emphasize key points and some pausing to regain attention.

The speaker is a leader. The audience expects to be led.

INTERESTING, NOT DULL

There are two principal ways to hold audience attention:

1. Captivate through vocal superiority and richness of language.
2. Speak to your listeners' needs and wants.

We must acknowledge that fame attracts too. Henry Kissinger is rumored to have recalled that as a university professor, he would go to parties, stand in the corner, and bore the few who would listen with his views on foreign policy. Then he became secretary of state. Did this make him a more interesting speaker? "Not really," Kissinger said. "Except now when I go to parties, people wait in line to be bored." Fame alone will attract, but it will not sustain prolonged interest.

Four Ways to *Sound* Interesting

Vocal Superiority

Chapter 8 will cover delivery and the voice in great detail. But let's note here that vocal quality and rhetorical skill—covered in chapter 9—can significantly boost listener interest. The tones and rhythms of accomplished speakers are compelling. Demagogues in all ages have used this knowledge to horrifying effect.

But you'll need a practiced voice to speak with an actor's grace and precision. The late Orson Welles appeared in a television advertisement in 1985 for Paul Masson Wines. When he intoned so low that "Paul Masson would sell no wine before its time," the very vines did shudder.

Helpful as a good voice may be, it will not carry you far if the topic is sober and your listeners critical. Still, only a fool would advise you to neglect your voice. Authorities who claim to be able to measure these things say that in some circumstances, the voice (sound, not content) carries nearly 40 percent of the speaker's "real" message. Of course, in a telephone conversation or other invisible communication this percentage can be even larger.

As the speech progresses in time, the words grow in importance because the audience becomes accustomed to, less distracted by, the speaker's voice and body. This it will do unless there are qualities of voice or body that the audience *can't* get used to (see chapter 8).

Richness of Language

How much content your words convey depends on how rich, or descriptive, they are. A rich word is vivid, specific, and definite. The communicative power of words also depends on the relevance, clarity, and immediacy of the thoughts they express.

Vivid Language

Much of what William Strunk and E. B. White say in their classic *The Elements of Style* is especially true of public speaking. In particular,

> If those who have studied the art of writing are in accord on any one point, it is on this: the surest way to arouse and hold the interest of the reader is by being specific, definite, and concrete. The greatest writers—Homer, Dante, Shakespeare—are effective largely because they deal in particulars and report the details that matter. Their words call up pictures.[29]

Vague:
We had enough to eat.

Definite:
We ate meat till our teeth fell out.

> —African tribesman referring to a water buffalo feast.

Vague:
The aircraft was out of control.

Definite:
The aircraft flew like "a piece of iron pipe thrown end for end."

> —TOM WOLFE, *The Right Stuff*

Abstract:
We must repair the city's infrastructure.

Concrete:
Our city needs work. The First Avenue Bridge is a relic, not fit for the horse carts that built it eighty years ago. We must also rebuild the seawall at the foot of Madison Street. Moreover,

twenty miles of the Hubbert Pipeline must be dug out of the muck and replaced—foot by dirty foot.

General:

The Soviet Union has effectively taken control of Eastern Europe.

Specific:

From Stettin in the Baltic to Trieste in the Adriatic, an iron curtain has descended across the continent.

> —WINSTON CHURCHILL, *May 5, 1946, Westminster College, Fulton, Missouri.*

Metaphors and Analogies

Dull speech comes from excessive generalization, and from too many words not grounded in the physical world. By contrast, interesting speakers take the life around them and use it. Metaphors and analogies are useful tools for this purpose because they simplify complex ideas and make abstract ideas concrete. They do this by matching the pattern of learning we follow all our lives long—constantly comparing and contrasting the familiar with the unfamiliar, seeking patterns to explain and demystify the things, people, and events around us. But just as well, they make a speaker *sound* interesting.

Ponderous:

When a woman rejects a man's advances, she may do so because she doesn't want to get involved with men. Or perhaps she does not care for that particular man.

Lively:

The man offering himself to a woman is like the waiter offering dessert. When the woman says no, it can mean she has no appetite for dessert. Or it can mean the dessert offered is not to her taste.

Ponderous:

One can attack either the symptoms or the disease. It is better to attack the disease.

Lively:

If you have a car, it probably comes with a light on the dash that will glow red when your engine overheats. Now, one thing you can do if that light comes on is hit it with a hammer you keep in the glove-box for just this purpose. Then you keep right on driving. This will work for a while. But soon the car will stop and you'll get out, look under the hood, and kick yourself for attacking the wrong problem. This is how most of us go through life—hitting the warning signs with a hammer while ignoring the real problems.

—CHARLES R. SWINDOLL, *on the radio ministry program "Insight for Living," September 28, 1988.*

Swindoll's commentary on smart motoring is not just a long-winded elaboration on a simple point. He has taken an important truth-turned-cliché and given it life by expressing it in concrete, familiar, and vivid language. That he has used considerably more words to do it is perfectly all right provided he has time to do it and provided the thought itself is worth it.

Ponderous:

During a recession, people tend to put off buying a new car. That causes the retention phase of the replacement cycle to become extended. But the cycle does continue and the public eventually returns to a buying phase.

Lively:

For a lot of people, buying a new car is like getting a haircut. When times are tough, they'll put it off for a while. But eventually, they get tired of looking like hell and they get it cut. It's the same with cars. They know they have to get one . . . it just takes them a little longer to get around to it.

—CHESTER A. COOK, *in a talk to a sales force, April 1983.*

Ponderous

I don't think this idea for more competition will work. They don't really want to compete, they just say they do. After a lot of commotion, things will go right back to where they were before.

More Lively:

Nobel Prize–winning scientist Konrad Lorenz said he was once out walking when he heard two dogs barking ferociously at one another. From the sound of it, Lorenz was certain the dogs would soon be tearing each other apart. But when he saw them, he was happy to find the dogs separated by a tall fence. Then suddenly, the dogs came to a large hole in the fence. They were nose to nose. This is it, Lorenz thought. But it wasn't. Instead of fighting to the death, the dogs retreated to the protection of a solid section of fence and resumed their belligerent displays, safe from direct confrontation.

So when we talk about removing the obstacles to competition, we must have realistic expectations.

Speaking of What Matters to the Listener

Be Relevant

Dale Carnegie put it bluntly years ago when he said that the average person is more concerned about his toothache than about the famine abroad. Carnegie's point was not that we are bad, or selfish, just human; what we find most interesting is what affects us directly.

So, if you want to make people like you, rule 5 is: Talk in terms of the other man's interests.[30]

The interests of speaker and listener do not always coincide. Mark Twain cautioned speakers, saying: "Don't complain and talk about all your problems. Eighty percent of the people won't care. The other 20 percent will think you deserve them."

This is a hard pill for many to swallow. Our corporate brethren, for example, routinely give the impression that they think the public is fascinated with their affairs when, in fact, they are not. The other day a local bank decided to change its name. To prepare for the expected deluge of inquiries and questions about this daring move, the bank installed twenty special phone lines and hired five temporary employees to cover them. The flood never came. The five operators took 42 calls in seven hours—total. That's 1.2 calls per person per hour. Good work if you can get it.

So what *do* people care about?

Speak to Their Needs

People have many needs. Which of these should the speaker be concerned about? Psychologist Abraham H. Maslow provided a key to the answer in his landmark book, *Motivation and Personality*, first published in 1954. Maslow's views on how our needs stand in relation to one another and how they affect our beliefs and actions (including our attention to speakers) have stood for thirty years. In this age of rapid scientific progress, that's a good record. If the speaker learns nothing else about human motivation, he should at least know about what Maslow called the hierarchy of needs.[31]

According to Maslow, there are five types of needs. They determine how people act, operating on the subconscious or unconscious level. The most basic needs are at the bottom of the pyramid. The most advanced, on the levels above.

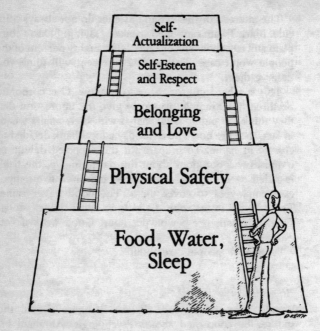

Maslow's Hierarchy of Needs

Why are these needs arranged in this order? Because, according to Maslow, only after the lower-level needs are satisfied do people seek to satisfy the higher. Which is why it never works to talk abstract art to a bunch of hungover, randy men at a tire dealers' convention—especially if there's a fire in the building. The converse should be noted—and this is where many speakers go lacking. If people have satisfied their physiological, safety, belonging, and self-esteem needs, they're searching for a lot more than two chickens in every pot. They're searching to make their lives meaningful. Not understanding this, many speakers aim too low, trying to motivate their listeners with promises of greater physical comfort when what they really want is greater self-esteem or a sense of belonging.

Maslow himself reminds us that the higher needs can sometimes override the physical needs. Some artists will endure every deprivation to continue to create, to self-actualize.

Appeals to freedom are powerful, Maslow says, because any impingement on our freedom—freedom of action, freedom of speech, freedom from arbitrary rule (justice)—lessens our ability to pursue *any and all* of our needs. This is why people are so easily moved by appeals to freedom. It's not that they're trying to satisfy a higher-order need for humanity in general; they're trying to protect themselves against having the means of satisfying their needs taken away.

In summary, a speech will be interesting if the content is relevant to the needs the listeners have at the moment—whether the listeners are conscious of those needs or not. At any given time, listeners can have multiple needs operating. And the higher-order needs can motivate as powerfully as the lower. As a parenthetical note, we must consider the influence of the American culture on Maslow's ordering of his needs. For example, had Maslow been Japanese, he may well have put the need to belong, to be accepted by society, higher than the need for self-actualization.

Being able to pick out what a listener needs *most* is key to using the persuasive principle of reframing discussed in chapter 4. And as we have seen in chapter 1, audience analysis is the key to discovering what those primary needs are.

Claims supported by appeals to different needs:

Appealing to a Physical Need	*Appealing to an Esteem Need*
Stop smoking. You'll ruin your health.	Stop smoking. You'll feel good about yourself.

Appealing to a Safety Need	*Appealing to a Belonging Need*
Drive a Mercedes. They protect you in a crash.	Drive a Mercedes. All the brokers at the firm do.

Appealing to Need for Love	*Appealing to Self-Actualization*
Give to the children's fund. They'll write you wonderful letters.	Give to the children's fund. It's doing the best you can.

Speak of the Immediate

People are interested in what's new, current, happening now. By talking about and referring to the latest developments, the speaker gains not only credibility, but also a certain authenticity.

Dull:

Home mortgage rates averaged 10.75% over the last month.

Interesting:

Just this morning, the Bailey Building and Loan dropped its home mortgage rate to 9 percent.

The current events to which a speaker refers may be directly related to the subject matter of the speech, or only tangentially related and brought up for the sake of illustration. For example, the following speech opening takes great advantage of current events to both ground the subject in contemporary life and to set the stage for important points to come.

> As we gather to discuss the battleground of health care, two great conflicts dominate the news—the Olympic Games in Seoul, South Korea, and the campaign for the presidency of the United States.
>
> The Olympics represent the best of all competitive worlds. The rules are strict. The judges are experts in their fields. But it is usually the unbiased clock that has the final say. Performance, and only performance, is what truly matters.
>
> Contrast the Olympics with the presidential campaign. As for rules, there are few. The judges—the voters—are not experts. And even they don't have the final say. The electoral college does. Actual candidate performance is secondary. How people feel about your performance is the *only* thing that matters.
>
> Now comes my question and my point. Consider the kind of competition you are in as nursing executives. Is it like the Olympics? Or like presidential politics?
>
> —IRMA GOERTZEN, *administrator, University of Washington Hospital, to the Health Care 1988 Conference, Milwaukee, Wisconsin, September 23, 1988.*

Speak of the Controversial

There's an old Irish saying: "If you want attention, start a fight." If you want attention as a speaker, talk about current conflicts. Or start one yourself. Emotions run hotter when ideas, events, and arguments are *polarized*—cast in terms of right or wrong, rich or poor; and *personified*—cast in terms of factions and their leaders. This isn't the most glorious human trait, but it's there.

Popular playwrights from Shakespeare to Miller to Simon to Mamet have built careers on the knowledge that conflict is the essence of drama. And a speech is a dramatic event.

Dull:

Teachers deserve higher pay and greater respect.

Interesting:

Why should we teachers be paid less than garbagemen? Why should we get less respect than dog-catchers, floor-waxers, or salespeople? Teachers deserve higher pay. We've earned greater respect. And we're going to fight every know-nothing legislator, every do-nothing administrator, every see-nothing reporter who stands in our way 'till we get it.

Summary

Sounding interesting and saying interesting things are the marks of captivating speakers. While sounding interesting is a matter of voice and language, saying interesting things is a function of speaking to the needs and passions of the listener.

Gimmicks and self-indulgence repel. Relevance and immediacy attract.

Part Two

DELIVERY

6

THE HARDWARE OF PUBLIC SPEAKING

Text, outlines, note cards, charts, props, visual displays—such is the hardware of public speaking. You must decide how much, if any of it, is necessary to build a satisfying presentation. (You'll need some materials to remember your speech and your listeners may benefit from well-made props and visual displays.)

But the materials you use to give a speech can impair as well as prepare. And the materials you select for the audience's benefit can confuse as well as clarify. So it pays to know the dos and don'ts.

The first don't is don't forget that you must create (or procure) and bring to the speaking site everything you'll use in your presentation. It's easy to be drained of energy and enthusiasm by last-minute efforts to create snappy visuals.

This chapter describes various kinds of speech hardware available to a wide range of speakers; it also prescribes their uses and describes their abuse.

YOUR SCRIPT

Whatever you use to remember your speech is a script. It can be word-for-word on many sheets of paper. It can be an outline of one form or other. It can be a set of note cards, each with some words on it. Or the script can be entirely internal, a memorized sequence of words and actions.

Your script should vary, depending on the formality of the occasion, your familiarity with the material, and your mental and physical comfort. A comfortable, well-versed speaker in an informal situation will prefer a few inconspicuous notes or may choose to rely on memory. An inexperienced speaker (or a careful one) in a formal situation may do best with a word-for-word script.

About Memorization

Work hard to commit the first fifteen seconds or so of your speech to memory. Have it written out in full, but try not to look at it unless you must. Knowing your opening lines cold will give you great confidence, helping you to open well. And as we've seen in earlier chapters, the opening is a crucial part of the speech.

You should be looking up when you deliver your first lines. You should be able to say those lines without stumbling or groping for words. And "winging it" during the opening is almost sure to get you into trouble. So plan out your opening, memorize it, and speak it as you've planned. If circumstances require some deviation from your plans, you'll know it early enough to rescript your opening and commit these changes to memory as well.

If you open well, odds are you'll keep doing well no

matter what kind of a script you rely on thereafter—until the closing. Many speeches fall apart at the end because the speaker hasn't preplanned a smooth conclusion. I urge you to do so. Further, I urge you to commit the last fifteen seconds of your speech to memory. That way, no matter what happens, you'll be able to exit gracefully.

But only the brave and foolish rely *totally* on memory. And then only for exceptionally formal occasions and for critical communications where relying on notes would undercut one's stature or credibility—as when asking for a raise or giving a toast.

Jack Valenti, President Lyndon Johnson's speechwriter and subsequently head of a large film distribution company, says that eight hundred words is about the maximum anyone can hope to memorize—about five minutes of material.

Few people have the discipline or need to memorize much of their speech. But most seriously, the stress of the speaking event itself can easily block recall. Forgetting just one word can cause some memorized performances to completely disintegrate, a terrible embarrassment to be avoided at all costs. So try to memorize your opening and closing statements—but have them written down just in case.

Four Kinds of Written Scripts and How to Use Them

Most speakers use one of four formats. To illustrate them, the same section of a speech has been rendered in four different ways. Many speakers will first write out a word-for-word script and then boil it down to something easier to handle at the podium.

The Word-for-Word Script	About Word-for-Word Scripts

EXAMPLE

Experts say there are four ways to *Sound Interesting.*

First, purge your speech of word-wimps. This means getting rid of words like "Utilize." "Heretofore." And "Really."

Second, be concrete. Add detail . . . detail that matters.

A *third* way to sound interesting . . . shorten your sentences. Remember that the ear is smaller than the mouth.

Fourth and finally, sound interesting by using vivid language . . . words that appeal to the eyes and ears . . . words that create images. Don't talk about dense forests. Talk about trees growing thick as fur on a squirrel.

How could anyone describe the Mt. St. Helens eruption and *not* recall the darkness at noon . . . or the sneezing horses?

COMMENT

Format

Ideally, the text should be in large type. Double-space between lines. Triple-space between paragraphs. Put the page number in the top right corner of every page. Only use the top two-thirds of the page. That will keep you from dropping your chin excessively (accentuating the appearance of reading) as you move down the page. End every page with a complete sentence.

How to Use Them

Practice reading it aloud many times. Edit carefully for smoothness and intelligiblity. Mark the script as you wish to remind yourself where to pause, emphasize, or vary your speaking rate. But don't clutter it.

When delivering your speech, follow this sequence of steps. Look at the script. Absorb a chunk. Look up and say that chunk to a specific person. Look down and absorb another chunk. Look up and deliver it.

Try not to talk as you look down for the next piece. Finish the one you're on while maintaining eye contact. When you're done with one page, slide it to one side, don't lift and turn it over—this is distracting and accentuates the appearance of reading. For those in politics or who find themselves taping a speech in a television studio, a TelePrompTer may come in handy. If you use one, be sure in rehearsal to get the machine to display your text at the proper pace.

Disadvantages

Beginning speakers are often advised to never use a word-for-word script. They are told it makes a speaker wooden and dull. This result is not inevitable. When full-text speeches are dull, it is usually not because they are delivered from texts per se, but because the speaker is not familiar with the text and/or the text itself is dull. Both these problems can be overcome with skill and practice. Some of the most stirring speeches ever given were written out word for word. Most audiences would vastly prefer an interesting speech delivered from a word-for-word script to a dull and rambling speech delivered off the cuff.

Full scripts do require a lectern that will accommodate two sheets of paper side by side. They require a speaker familiar enough with the text to talk it, not read it. And that calls for the ability to write in conversational language. A good script also takes a great deal of time to prepare.

Advantages

The speaker is assured of saying *exactly* what is planned, and need not worry about forgetting anything—it's all there. Additionally, there's little worry about running short or long.

The Traditional Outline

EXAMPLE

I. 4 Ways to Sound Interesting
   A. GET RID OF
      WORD-WIMPS
      1. Utilize
      2. Heretofore
      3. Really
   B. BE CONCRETE
      Add detail that
      matters.

About Traditional Outlines

COMMENT

Format

The traditional outline format is useful to a point. If overdone, the outline's symbols can distract, rather than aid comprehension and recollection. As with full-text, use only the top two-thirds of each

C. SHORTEN SENTENCES
   Ear Smaller than
   Mouth
D. USE VIVID LANGUAGE
   1. Words that appeal to
      eyes, ears
   2. Words that Create
      Images
   Example:
   "Trees as thick as fur
   on a squirrel."
   Example:
   Mt. St. Helens blast
   · darkness at noon
   · sneezing horses

page. Again, page numbers
should be put at the top right
so the speaker will know immediately if the pages are out
of order without having to
search the page for content.
Use black ink on white paper.

Disadvantages

Without discipline, it's easy
to overtalk some points, under-
talk others, talk too long or too
short. Traditional outlines can
be very hard to follow, especially when too much is on a
page. They open greater opportunity for slips of the
tongue, gaffes, and losing
one's place.

Advantages

They allow for more spon-
taneity. They reduce the size
and/or volume of paper the
speaker must control and organize at the podium.

The Key-Word Outline

EXAMPLE

Four Ways to Sound Interesting

· NO WORD-WIMPS

About Key-Word Outlines

COMMENT

Format

Take from a completed outline or full text those key
words that will jog loose an entire thought, example, or sup-

· BE CONCRETE

· SHORT SENTENCES

· VIVID LANGUAGE

Squirrel

Mt. St. Helens

porting analogy. Arrange these words in the order that the thoughts they represent are to be expressed. Numerals and other symbols of organization are unnecessary. Write key words boldly with a black marker on a white background.

How to Use

Glance at the word, recall the thought, look up and talk it. When finished with that thought, look down at the next key word, and so on.

Disadvantages

They offer little help to a failing memory. They invite rambling and sloppy wording.

Advantages

They offer the speaker freedom and encourage spontaneity. They are preferred for all informal speaking because they are the least obtrusive. An entire speech can be outlined on a few four-by-six note cards and, with practice, on one. The speaker does not need a podium or lectern, but can easily hold the outline in one hand.

The Pictograph

EXAMPLE

About Pictographs

COMMENT

Format

Each of these simple pictures, like hieroglyphics, has a specific meaning assigned by the speaker. Unlike hieroglyphics, each picture should represent not just a word or phrase but an entire idea or series of ideas. Simply arrange them in order of delivery. Most important is that the speaker draw the pictures. This will vastly increase his or her chances of recalling its precise meaning. Moreover, in drawing the pictograph, the speaker will be rehearsing and refining the speech with every pen stroke. Use a black felt-tip pen on white paper.

How to Use

Look at one symbol long enough to understand the thoughts it represents. Look up and speak the thoughts.

Disadvantages

In the heat of the moment, it can be easy to forget what the pictures stand for. They allow

for rambling and can lead to
poor use of the time available.
Some ideas resist depiction.
Sometimes, many pictures are
needed, requiring many pages.

Advantages

If you have highly devel-
oped visual and tactile senses,
you may find drawings far
easier to use than text or outlines. This form of script is the
most liberating of all because it
suggests no specific words at
all—just ideas.

VISUAL AIDS, PROPS, AND HANDOUTS

Making a sales presentation, leading a professional semi-
nar, giving a progress report to management, presenting a
zoning plan to the city council, or explaining how boats
are built—all are situations that call for more than words.
They cry out for materials to aid listener comprehension
and appreciation, such as graphs, pictures, props, and
handouts.

The attraction many speakers feel toward visual aids and
props can be traced directly to elementary school show-and-
tell. Clutching a sackful of pine cones or turtle eggs, the
youngster doesn't feel quite so naked standing in front of
his or her peers. Many chief executives stage multimedia
extravaganzas for this very reason.

If the purpose of visual materials is not to support the speaker's ideas but rather to divert the audience's attention, a steep price will be paid. The first cost is the expense of the materials themselves, which can be substantial in terms of both time and money. The second cost is to the prestige of the speaker-presenter. When the slide show *becomes* the message, the speaker is reduced to an audiovisual technician—a role which the speaker does not want and for which he or she is probably transparently unqualified. With speeches, as with everything else, every new layer of complexity increases the odds that something will go wrong.

Even the most simple visual aid is potentially a trap in waiting. This was unintentionally illustrated by President Reagan on the night of April 29, 1982. The economy foundering, Reagan came on live national television to make a highly publicized presentation on his administration's efforts to curb inflation and control federal spending. Partway into an explanation of his programs, Reagan produced a large display card on which a bar graph of budgetary data had been drawn earlier. Reagan's plan was to complete the graph on live television, adding drama and emphasis. Things didn't go as planned. Picking up the marking pen at the critical moment, the president made the proper motion, dragging the marker across the card. But no marks came forth, only squeaks. The pen was as dry as Calvin Coolidge. Clearly upset, Reagan ad-libbed, "I can't seem to make a mark big enough." After some fumbling, a disembodied hand pushed a new marking pen across the table, whereupon the president grabbed it and resumed the lesson. And the world said to itself, "The leader of the most powerful country on earth can't operate a felt-tip pen."

Flip Charts

These are devices for holding erect a multisheet pad of drawing paper. Most common is the free-standing tripod affair that comes with a tray for pens and a bracket of some sort to hold the paper pad in place. They also come in smaller sizes which can be placed on a conference table, suitable for smaller groups.

How to Prepare

1. Buy your own pad and prepare your visuals beforehand. The best pads to use have thick, white paper (so markers won't bleed through to next page) and a faint grid pattern to help make lettering uniform.

2. Arrange drawings in order of use, the first in front.

3. Use billboard-style graphics: short, simple words, bold lettering, a few bright colors. Use broad-nib felt-tip pens for easy recognition. To display statistical information, use simple pie charts, bar charts, and line graphs.

Remember—and this goes for all visual formats—presenting information visually is *more* than writing key words and numbers on paper. The best visuals are ones that express ideas pictorially—by graphic comparisons of quantities or by drawings of objects.

4. Every page bearing a chart, graph, summary of points, whatever, should bear only one and be boldly titled—for the speaker's as well as the audience's benefit.

5. Make certain your speaking site has a flip-chart stand available and that your pad will fit onto the pegs or under the clamp provided. I always take masking tape along just in case the pad doesn't fit and I have to secure it some other way.

These Present Information Visually	These Do Not

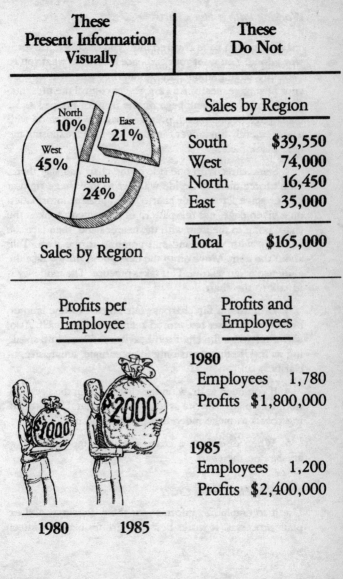

Sales by Region

Sales by Region

South	$39,550
West	74,000
North	16,450
East	35,000
Total	$165,000

Profits per Employee

Profits and Employees

1980
Employees 1,780
Profits $1,800,000

1985
Employees 1,200
Profits $2,400,000

1980   1985

Working with a Flip Chart

1. Keep each page covered until you discuss it. Cover it when done. You want your audience looking at what you're currently talking about, not wondering what the stuff on your next page means. An easy way to control the presentation is to leave a blank page on the front of the pad and a blank page between each prepared page. When done with a page, merely flip it over the top of the stand, exposing the next blank page.

2. Stand directly to one side of the chart and stay there. Don't force them to decide whether to look stage right at you or stage left at your chart. To emphasize information on a given page, use this pattern of movement: look at the chart, point to the item with the nearer hand, then face the audience with your hand still pointing to the item. Talk about the item. Move on to the next point. *Always* face the audience when talking. This takes practice. The tendency is to talk to the chart.

3. Don't use a flip chart as your notes. No one is interested in your notes but you, so keep them to yourself. Also, if you rely on a flip chart too heavily, you'll end up speaking to it. Use flip charts only to accentuate, emphasize, or clarify.

4. If you need to draw on the charts during the presentation, take pains to write as legibly as you can. Use alternating colors to make individual points stand out.

5. When discussing a chart, use the same language as appears on the chart.

When to Use a Flip Chart

Use it to emphasize information, show drawings, and explain processes. It works best with groups between fifteen and forty and as a change of pace in longer presentations. An excellent apparatus for engaging the audience in discussion and/or focusing their attention.

Overhead Projectors

This electrically powered projection device uses plastic film transparencies measuring approximately ten inches by twelve inches. Weighing in at around fifteen pounds, the machine casts an enlarged reproduction of the film image onto a smooth, vertical surface—most commonly a wall. Best results are achieved in a darkened room. However, unlike the slide projector, many overhead projectors will work with subdued indoor lighting provided the apparatus is close enough to the wall onto which you're projecting the information.

How to Prepare

1. Draw what you want on your transparencies in advance of the speech. You can buy blank ones from most office-supply stores. Many large companies stock them in their supplies centers. Special markers are required for drawing. Machines can be purchased which thermographically transfer images from regular paper to the transparency film itself.

2. The same graphics rules for flip charts apply here: simple layouts, headlines for each transparency, use of bright colors, use of graphs to display relationships among numbers. Try mightily to avoid mere lists of words and numbers.

3. When things go wrong with overhead projectors, it's usually one of three things, all preventable: a cord not long

enough to properly position the machine, a projection lens support arm that won't adjust, or a projection lamp that's burned out.

Working with Overhead Projectors

1. Stand to side of machine. Lay transparency on projection surface or enlist a confederate to lay them down for you. You'll need a table to keep used ones separate from the ordered stack in waiting.

2. Use a pointer. A pencil will do (the hand is too large and will obscure too much of the image). Touch your pointer to the material you want to indicate—do this on the transparency itself.

3. Arrange your points so that you can keep the ones which have not been discussed covered with a sheet of paper until you're ready to discuss them.

4. Number each transparency boldly on the cardboard frame, not on the film, and reference each by number in your notes. This will help prevent disorganization and fumbling during the presentation.

5. Turn the machine off when not displaying information. The glare is strong and the fan noise can be loud—both are distracting.

When to Use Overhead Transparencies

They work best for medium-sized audiences of thirty to seventy people. Overhead projection is a much less restrictive medium than slide projection. You can easily change the order of your transparencies and, though it is not easy to do, it is at least possible to write new things on them during your speech. This can't be done with slides. However, unlike slides, they will not project a photographic-quality image, so, like flip charts, they are best used for simple graphs and line drawings.

Travelling executives like them because carrying a set of transparencies is much easier than lugging a flip chart through an airport. It takes practice to draw on a transparency while it is laying on the projector. Also, a speaker operating an overhead projector is much more a prisoner of the medium while it is on—they are obtrusive and clunky and the glare is hard on the speaker's eyes.

Slide Projectors

Projectors for 35mm slides vary greatly in style and capability. This wide variety notwithstanding, the speaker will most often encounter a simple machine with a single, circular, carousel tray which will hold (and lock in place) up to one hundred slides. Depending on quality, slide machines will project with great clarity over a distance of many yards to a resulting screen dimension up to hundreds of square feet.

How to Prepare

1. Slides can be taken by the speaker with a 35 mm camera, bought ready-made, generated by special attachments for personal computers, or created to order by specialty houses.

2. Preview all tentative selections with a projector. Embarrassing details can appear out of nowhere once the slide is on the wall. A friend of mine once put together an informational slide presentation for the director of marketing of a large medical group. The purpose of the presentation was to inform the listener-viewers of the completeness of the services offered by the organization as well as to portray the

organization as technologically up-to-date. A slide showing an ambulance in front of the emergency entrance to a hospital was selected to portray the ability to handle traumatic injuries. So far so good. But once on the wall, the image cast was not of a technologically up-to-date facility—the ambulance in the picture was a good thirty years old and the driver's clothing and hair style were positively laughable. These details could not be seen in the small image of the slide held in the hand.

3. Graphics rules for flip charts and overheads apply here also, particularly the need to transform all statistical information into simple graphs. Slides crowded with excessive detail (tables of numbers especially) only create listener fatigue and annoyance.

4. Number slides on their cardboard frames by order of appearance. Arrange slides in the tray. Many trays have a locking cover to prevent the slides from spilling out. Reference the slide numbers in your notes just in case.

5. Use them sparingly. We've all suffered through tedious slide presentations which use five slides to do the job of one.

6. Meticulously check and double-check all details of operation. Make certain that the room will darken. Enlist a confederate to operate the room lights for you. Get there well in advance to check the setup of the machine or do it yourself. Don't seat listeners next to the machine—they won't be able to hear you over the fan noise. Run through your slides once at the site, learning all the operations of the machine—how to advance slides and reverse direction, how to work the remote control pad (if any), and how to change the projection bulb. A spare is commonly inside the machine case. If not, it's a good idea to have an extra that will fit that particular machine.

Working with a Projector

1. Ideally, stand to one side of the images projected on the wall or screen. This keeps the audio (your voice) coming from the area of the picture. Plus, it reminds the audience that this is *your* presentation. Use a remote-control pad to operate the machine. Use a pointer to emphasize items of interest on the slide. Don't play with the pointer or you'll remind the audience of General Patton.

2. Since the room will be dark, you'll need a small lamp to see your notes. A podium with a light is best, but not always available. And because you'll be speaking far from your listeners and because the projector is noisy even after turned off (the fan keeps running to cool the machine), you'll probably need a microphone.

3. The projector should be off when you start your speech. And it should be off when you conclude your speech. Remember—you are in control. Not the machine. Your *ideas* are the message. The slides only illustrate and emphasize.

4. For important presentations, have a backup machine and a technician available in case the machine should stop working during your presentation.

When to Use Slides

Try not to show slides directly after lunch or dinner. When the room darkens, people tend to fall asleep.

Use only with a large group—sixty and up—unless the visuals are vital and cannot be shown any other way. For example, a lecture on art history will benefit greatly from slides of artwork and there is virtually no other way to show art to many people at a time except by slides.

Slides are the least interactive of all supportive media,

meaning that they increase the psychological distance between speaker and audience.

From both a presentation and preparation standpoint, slides are the most complicated of all the visual media, and therefore the most risky.

Props

Any three-dimensional object used to illustrate or emphasize is a prop. For example, during a speech on oil drilling techniques, an executive once filled a drinking glass with a mixture of gravel, sand, and molasses to illustrate how newly discovered oil is not normally found in pools of pressurized liquid, but rather in sticky globs of muck deep in the earth. He then worked two straws into his glass of muck to illustrate how the oil is extracted. One "straw," he said, is used to pump pressurized steam into the muck. This liquifies and pressurizes the oil. The other "straw" is used to carry the steam-driven oil to the surface.

A prop can clarify what words cannot. Props are far superior to visual displays for conveying tactile information and showing how things work. They can be vital to sales presentations.

How to Prepare

Easy. Just bring it to the speech or presentation.

Working with Props

1. Keep them hidden from audience view until use, then put them away. Bring the prop out after the speech for people to examine.

2. If your prop is something you must demonstrate, make sure it works *every* time; and rehearse your every move and

every word. "Well, it usually works" is a singularly unconvincing demonstration.

When to Use Props

Use props to add life to dull or complex subjects. Unless your prop is quite large, the issue of visibility requires restriction to small groups. Unless your speech is one to entertain, resist the strong urge toward slapstick. While humor is a useful tool, props in bad taste can irreparably diminish a speaker's credibility. Be especially careful with props that must be worn. Anything you put on your body has the effect of saying, "This is who I really am."

Videotape

Coupled with small- and large-screen monitors, videocassette playback decks are no longer public speaking novelties. Videotaped minibiographies were used at both the Democratic and Republican national conventions in 1988 as a way to build crowd enthusiasm immediately prior to the acceptance speeches of their newly nominated candidates for the presidency. They were tremendously effective, far more so than the traditional speech of introduction.

But for the everyday speaker, videotape is still too expensive to produce and edit to be practical. However, it won't always be. When quality production equipment is available, the speaker must *still* weigh all the standard considerations about visual aids in deciding the place of videotape in the presentation: Is it relevant, is it informative, is it entertaining, is it worth the trouble?

Videotape has no equal when it comes to illustrating that most complex subject of all—people. For example, nothing more effectively illustrates the principles of speech delivery than a variety of clips of public speakers in action.

There are two chief dangers in using videotape. First,

because you're operating in the same medium as television, the viewer is likely to expect the same quality—and usually won't get it. Second, if the listeners wanted to watch a screen, they might well have stayed home. But they didn't. They came to see and hear you. Make sure they have ample opportunity to do both.

Also important is proper editing and queuing of the tape, so the observer is not made to watch several seconds or minutes of extraneous material before the right stuff appears.

Handouts

How to Prepare

Quality should be as high as time and money allow. It is much better to provide a single, colorful, well-done page which summarizes and clarifies the main points of the speech than dump on the listener ten pages of poorly reproduced source documents.

How to Use Handouts

1. The general rule is not to hand out printed materials before or during the speech. People tend to look at the handouts rather than listen to the speaker. If you want them to follow along with the main points, it's much better to use a flip chart or an overhead projector because you have control over what they see and when they see it.

2. *Do not* leave handouts on the banquet tables or chairs unless your listeners will have plenty of time to satisfy their curiosity about the contents well before you speak. You don't want them to miss your important ideas because their heads are buried in your handouts. Few things are as unset-

tling to speakers as having their audience reading when they should be listening. Station a confederate at the exit door to disperse the material after your speech, or mail it, or leave it, for example, with the legislator's assistant, or with the purchasing manager's secretary.

When to Use Handouts

The most important handout reminds the listener how to respond to a speech to activate. It lists relevant names, addresses, phone numbers—all those things the listener wanted to write down during the speech but couldn't.

When the speech is a sales presentation, leave literature. When the speech presents a staff report, leave a one-page summary. If you like, make the full report available on request.

Finally, consider preparing handouts as a backup in the event that your slide projector or overhead projector fails you at the scene.

7

ATTITUDES, NERVES, AND REHEARSAL

Many people are afraid of giving speeches. And many who aren't probably should be. For every introvert fighting back terror to recall his meticulously prepared speech, two extroverts boldly go where no thought has gone before.

Luckily, people can and do adapt to the stresses of speech making. They develop self-confidence. They learn self-control. They come to understand and respect their listeners. They become excellent speakers. It is a beautiful sight when a timid soul crosses the threshold from obscurity to recognition. It's just as beautiful when a wild soul becomes focused, acquiring the mantle of substance. This chapter is about becoming psychologically prepared to deliver a speech.

Besides actually writing your speech, there are three parts to effective preparation:

1. Developing rational expectations and helpful attitudes.
2. Understanding and learning to control the physiology and psychology of stress.
3. Rehearsing—mentally and physically.

ATTITUDES AND EXPECTATIONS

While running a workshop on public speaking a few years ago, I decided to broach the problem of performance anxiety. I asked nine people, some men, some women, to tell me what they feared most about speech making. What they kindly told me was, if not comprehensive, certainly representative of the fears that commonly afflict public speakers. Here is what they feared:

- I'll make a horrible mistake.
- They'll walk out.
- They'll see through me and realize I don't know what I'm talking about.
- I'll forget what I have to say and fall apart.
- They'll be people who dislike people like me.
- My voice will crack and I'll be humiliated.
- They'll heckle me and try to embarrass me.
- They'll ask me something I don't know.
- My speech will bore them.
- I'll freeze—won't be able to continue.
- I'll leave my speech at home or go to the wrong room.
- They'll have heard it all before.
- I'll wet my pants or throw up.
- I'll lose my temper and yell at them.

We divided this list in two—one for fears about the audience, another for fears about ourselves. Of each fear listed we asked, Is this realistic? If it wasn't, we wrote down what was. If there was some basis to the fear, we wrote our best guess of what would happen if the fear was realized. Here is the result of our investigation.

Fears About the Audience

Fear	*Realistic Appraisal*
They'll walk out.	Some people may leave before I'm through. But that doesn't necessarily mean they don't like me. They may have a prior engagement or an emergency.
They'll see through me.	They'll think I mean what I say unless I give them some reason to think otherwise. If I'm prepared, they'll be impressed with my knowledge and organization.
They'll dislike people like me.	Most people are not bigoted. Those that are are misguided and need help.
They'll heckle me.	Heckling is very rare. Few audiences will tolerate hecklers anyway.
They'll ask me something I don't know.	I don't know all the answers. Who does? If I'm asked a question I can't answer, I'll say, "I don't know the answer to that question."
They'll have heard it all before.	Maybe they have heard some of it before. That will only add credibility to my message. But most of what I have to say is new because it is what I think.

Fear	*Realistic Appraisal*
They won't be convinced.	Some will be convinced, some won't. It depends on how good a job I do as well as what they already believe. I can only control how I perform, so I'll do my best.

Fears About Myself

Fear	*Realistic Appraisal*
I'll make a horrible mistake.	I probably will make *at least* one mistake. Everybody does. It will seem bigger to me than it will to the audience. And I'll go on.
I'll forget what I have to say and fall apart.	I may well forget what I want to say at some point in my speech. But if I do forget, I'll look at my notes and remember. In any event, it's highly doubtful that I'll fall apart.
My voice will crack and I'll be humiliated.	My voice may crack. It can happen if my throat is too tight from nervousness. I'll do some relaxation exercises before I start and remember to breathe deeply. If my voice does crack, I'll be embarrassed, but I'll go on.
I'll freeze and won't be able to continue.	I must remember that time seems to stand still when

Fear	*Realistic Appraisal*
	my adrenaline is pumping from nervousness. What seems like an eternity of silence to me probably just seems like a thoughtful pause to the audience. I probably won't freeze if I'm well prepared and can pick out a friendly face in the audience to talk to.
I'll leave my speech at home or go to the wrong place.	I'll ask a friend who's going to my speech to carry an extra copy for me should I forget, which is highly unlikely. To make certain that I get to the right place, I'll make a reconnaissance run ahead of time or engage a knowledgeable confederate to guide me there on the day.
I'll have an accident.	If I honestly feel that I might throw up or lose control of my bladder, I should see a doctor about it and seriously consider not giving the speech. No speech is worth losing my health or my self-respect.
I'll lose my temper and yell at someone.	If I'm frightened enough, I might raise my voice in self-defense. That's OK. I'll calm down after that. I will try to remember that a rush of adrenaline can

Fear	*Realistic Appraisal*
	make frightening things seem worse than they really are.
I'll be bored and it will show.	If I am bored with the material, I'll work hard not to show it. And I'll try to find some peppier material. After that, it's their responsibility. I've done my part.

If a speaker believes the audience is basically friendly, intelligent, and fair-minded . . . if a speaker believes he or she is well prepared, feels happy to have the opportunity to speak, and is confident of the ability to recover from mistakes . . . if a speaker feels this way, odds are great that the speaker will be well received, will deliver the speech well, and enjoy the outing tremendously.

But what of the speaker who believes the audience is hostile, stupid, and there to humiliate? What of the speaker who feels ill-prepared, who is unhappy about having to speak, and has little confidence in his or her ability to bounce back from errors? It is safe to say the odds are good that this speaker will do poorly and feel miserable before, during, and after.

Developing an upbeat attitude means learning to control self-talk, the voice inside that can make things appear much worse than they are. The surest remedy for a hang-dog attitude is unrelenting preparation. If you work hard on a speech, pretty soon you just have to tell someone about it or you'll bust.

NERVES

Feeling happy and self-assured is difficult when our vocal cords seem frozen and our knees have taken on the stability of warm pudding. People with little experience with speaking before groups and, for that matter, those with a great deal at stake, can quite literally be overcome by the shock of public speaking. Fortunately, there are proven means of prevention. To gain control over nervous anxiety and fear, it is helpful to understand the biological mechanisms involved in producing them.

The Alarm Reaction

Hans Selye was the first to comprehensively describe the psycho-biological mechanisms behind what for centuries has been called stage fright. Today, because of Selye's work, we call it the alarm reaction.

In the *Handbook on Stress and Anxiety,* Selye describes the process in this way:

The alarm reaction is a sequence of physiological events set off when we enter *what we judge* to be a stressful situation.

The first phase of the alarm reaction is shock. This is characterized by:

- increased heart rate.
- loss of muscle tone.
- decreased core temperature.
- lowered blood pressure.

The second phase is countershock, where the body works to stabilize the vital signs. This is the job of the adrenal glands, and some nerve endings themselves, which release stimulating hormones. The most well-known of these is adrenaline, "secreted to make available energy, to accelerate the pulse rate, to elevate blood pressure and the rate of blood circulation in the muscles, and to stimulate the central nervous system," according to Selye. The adrenaline response is instantaneous.[32]

Every speaker goes through this cycle—at various levels of intensity. The more severe the shock phase, the harder the body must work to counter it to give the speaker the presence of mind needed to deliver a good speech. When people faint it is because their body literally can't take the stress—can't overcome the shock response quickly enough to stabilize the vital signs. If the stress is prolonged, other hormones—cortisones—are called up to maintain long-term arousal. The severity of the alarm reaction depends, in all of its phases, on how threatening we judge the situation to be. What merely excites one person may panic another. The difference in reaction is a matter of experience with similar situations (whether real or simulated) and the mental conditioning that comes from them.

Coping with the Shock-Adrenaline Response

Knowing how the stress reaction works, we are led to a few important conclusions about how to cope with it.

1. Understand that the alarm reaction is manageable. It can be controlled. How weak you feel at the onset of the speech or how fast your heart beats is literally up to you. Franklin Roosevelt's classic statement, "We have nothing to fear but fear itself," is an excruciatingly accurate description of the perils of stage fright.

Dorothy Sarnoff, accomplished stage actress and author of the insightful book on public speaking, *Make the Most of*

Your Best, writes the following advice regarding stage fright:

> The muscles of your vital triangle control nervousness because the solar plexus, one of the major nerve-control centers of your body, lies behind that triangle. It affects production of adrenaline—the chemical that galvanizes you for action with positive nervousness. But the solar plexus also can produce noradrenaline or norepinephrine, the chemical that makes you panic.
>
> Contracting the vital triangle muscles reduces or stops the production of norepinephrine.[33]

Unfortunately, what Sarnoff says here has little basis in fact. The solar plexus, a bundle of nerves behind the stomach and in front of the aorta, may stimulate the parasympathetic, or calming, nervous system. But it has little to do with the production or regulation of either adrenaline or norepinephrine. However, the fact that the premise of her prescription is dubious doesn't make her vital triangle (diaphragm muscles) contraction exercise (consciously tightening the abdominal muscles, then relaxing them—or having someone hug you forcefully under your rib cage from behind) less effective.

2. Do your homework on the audience. Realistically assess your ability to cope with them. Don't assume anything. Remember that the harshness of the alarm reaction depends greatly on how threatening you *believe* the situation to be.

3. Become so thoroughly familiar with the opening of your speech that you can deliver it under duress. Getting through the first few sentences unscathed has a wonderful calming effect.

4. Accept your body's reaction to stress as normal and beneficial. Be assured that such discomforts as a fluttering heartbeat, clammy hands, tight throat, jelly knees, flushed

face, and a feeling that time is flying will pass as your shock
defenses kick in and you get a clearer reading of the audience.

5. If you worry about being overcome by panic, schedule
a time to panic well before the speech. Get it out of the way.
Then continue calmly with your preparation. It sounds silly,
but it works.

6. Learn to relieve and reduce those symptoms of stress
that impair speech the most. Here are a few tips:

· Move. If you feel your body becoming rigid, move.
Move anything—hands, arms, feet—just move. It's a good
idea to plan a few simple gestures into your opening remarks.

· Here's a simple exercise you can do anywhere to
loosen muscles in you throat, chest, jaw and brow: First,
mentally assign that tenseness to your hands. Picture it
there. Make fists and squeeze as hard as you can (or grip the
podium) for five seconds. Then relax.

· Follow Sophie Tucker's advice on living a long life:
Keep breathing. Take a few *deep* breaths before you begin.
Part of the shock response is rapid and shallow breathing—
too much of which will cause you to black out. And pushing
down on the diaphragm will calm you down.

· Dry mouth can be helped by tucking a clove (the spice)
or hard candy between your cheek and gums.

· Stand with your knees slightly bent. This will help
circulation in your legs, promoting a feeling of solidity and
well-being.

· If you feel your throat tightening, *do not* clear it repeatedly. This will tighten your vocal cords even further. Take
a drink of water instead. In fact, drink lots of water the day

before your speech. Keeping your body well hydrated will give your voice more resilience.

· Avoid drinking milk in the hours preceding a speech. It coats your throat, and will make you want to clear it often.

· This will be hard for coffee drinkers, but try not to drink much of it during the twelve hours prior to your speech. It tightens the throat. Alcoholic beverages have the same unfortunate effect. Mild, noncaffeinated tea does a good job relaxing the throat.

· If you're the after-dinner speaker, be especially careful *not* to eat much at the prespeech meal. It will dull your mind because so much blood will be diverted to the task of digestion.

· If at all possible, get plenty of sleep the night before. Fully rested, you'll be better able to maintain a positive attitude and your body will be better able to marshall your countershock responses.

· Giving a speech of any kind places a high demand on the systems—mental and physical. It helps tremendously to be in good physical and mental condition.

Well, you say, "This is all very good, but what if I *still* black out?" On that, I can only recount what happened to astronaut Gulon Bluford, Jr., during his keynote speech at the June 8, 1984, commencement ceremonies of Thomas Jefferson University in Philadelphia. About twenty minutes into it, he collapsed in front of 2,200 people, an apparent victim of nervousness and hot lighting overhead. After a few minutes, Bluford returned to the podium to a standing ovation, joked that his next engineering degree would be in air-conditioning, and finished his speech.

The vast majority of audiences *want* the speaker to succeed because they understand full well the difficulty involved.

ELEMENTS OF EFFECTIVE REHEARSAL

A speech may be many things, but when its over, you're done. You don't get a second chance, at least not for a while and perhaps never with the same audience on the same subject. In this way, speech making is similar to running a race. When the pistol pops, you want to be at the peak of your ability. Since every speech and every speaker is unique, no single readiness routine will do for all. But here are some techniques used by experienced speakers:

1. Say your entire speech aloud at least once. If you can, stand up while doing it. Some people are aided by having a rehearsal audience. Some aren't. Try both. One accomplished speaker I know practices delivering her speeches while driving—she likes not having to worry that she might be overheard. And it forces her to commit key parts to memory since she can't easily consult her notes while navigating in traffic.

2. Say your entire speech at bedtime the night before. With nothing else going on to compete for memory space, your speech will more easily enter long-term memory.

3. If you have any humorous stories or anecdotes in your speech, practice telling them to people who won't be present at the talk.

4. If you can, make a reconnaissance trip to the site. While there, practice your opening and closing. Get com-

fortable in the setting. Take notes about whatever needs doing to prepare the site for your presentation.

5. In the few minutes just preceding your talk, try a visualization exercise like the following:

> Recall your hours of preparation and planning. Remember how careful you were to select the right clothes for the occasion—and how good you look in the mirror. When it's time to go on, see yourself smiling, walking tall and confidently, walking smoothly to your place. Feel yourself breathing easily, throat relaxed as you stand solidly, self-assuredly facing the audience, eager to begin.
>
> See yourself looking at many friendly people in the audience; see them looking at you and smiling, recognizing your right to the stage. Hear yourself starting your speech with a firm voice, using the same words you practiced earlier. Watch the many faces of recognition and approval in the audience as you smoothly make the transition into the body of your speech.
>
> Listen to yourself developing your points with confidence. Feel your energy rising and see your listeners paying keen attention as you begin your concluding statements. When you say your final words, feel the joy of accomplishment. See yourself standing confidently for a few well-earned seconds to soak up the applause and good feeling.
>
> Listen to the applause as you take your seat. Feel pride for having met a tough challenge with intelligence, dignity and caring.

Summary

1. Listen to what you say to your mind's ear. Replace faulty, catastrophic ideas about yourself and your audience with accurate, positive ideas.

2. Attack and control physical rigidity through preventive measures and tension-reducing exercises.

3. Calm yourself and focus your energy through supportive visualization.

4. Force yourself to do a good a job because it's important. Believe in the value of your message and the strength of your preparation. Remember the *purpose* of your speech. Believe in yourself.

8

ELEMENTS OF
EFFECTIVE
PRESENTATION

What's the best way to give a speech? Your way. There are some boundaries and some things not to do. But a tremendous range of physical and vocal behavior is allowed and even encouraged.

It's easy to feel we must reach the level of a professional performer before anyone will pay attention. This just isn't true. People have been moved and inspired, educated and entertained by a vast range of personalities, voices, and bodies.

After you get a feel for the dos and don'ts, get out there and enjoy it. A speech gives shy people full license to try on a new personality for a few minutes. Many actors are self-professed introverts. In fact, naturally extroverted people generally have a more difficult time in the body language and voice department than introverted people. I believe this follows from the tendency of most introverts to be highly self-monitoring and for extroverted people to be generally less self-monitoring. (*Self-monitoring* is what psychologists say we're doing when we're conscious of how our actions are affecting others.) Because they are more aware of how they behave at the podium, introverted people can more easily identify bad habits and change them.

This doesn't mean that extroverts can't improve their considerable communication abilities. They can, by learning to be more self-aware. Anyone who wishes to improve his speech enjoyment and effectiveness will benefit greatly from watching a videotape of himself giving a speech. It's best to do this in the company of a *knowledgeable* supporter.

Even the most polished delivery cannot match the persuasive punch of raw determination. I had an excellent debate partner in school who had a form of epilepsy. At tournaments, Frank would be fine until he got sleepy. Then the tremors would start. At the end of a long tournament we'd really be dragging, having debated perhaps six times in two days, along with competing in any individual events we might have entered. We got about as much sleep at night as you'd expect for teenagers bunking together in an out-of-town motel.

It was not uncommon for Frank to be talking away and then go into a trance, grip the podium, and shake a little. That would go on for fifteen seconds or so and then he'd come out of it—like somebody switched him on again, he'd pick up right where he left off. I always thought of Frank's attacks as a secret weapon; they certainly proved the effectiveness of pausing. Thanks, Frank.

NONVERBAL COMMUNICATION IN GENERAL

Hollywood studio executives in the early 1920s were desperately worried that movies would not survive the invention of the sound track. Their fears stemmed from the knowledge that the voices of many silent screen stars did not match their nonverbal personalities. A suave Casanova peeping like Betty Boop would not do; neither would a femme fatale barking like a fishmonger. The movies survived, but most silent screen stars did not. The clash between the sound of their voices and their film personas was too great for the viewing public.

This page from Hollywood history illustrates a major point about communication:

> Effective communication depends on consistency among all the component parts of the message. In public speaking, these components are four: the words spoken, the voice that speaks them, the face and eyes, and the body.

Angry words whispered from smiling lips make an eerie presentation indeed. But more important, it is confusing. When the picture in the newspaper doesn't match the caption below it, we are annoyed.

When your facial expressions, tone of voice, and bodily posture say one thing and your words say another, the words are discounted. Experience teaches us that what matters most in these situations of incongruity is the emotional content. To get it we read body language. Emotional content includes such things as whether the message is happy or sad, serious or light-hearted, urgent or meant for casual consideration. Our perception of the emotional content of a message also includes assessment of the speaker's conviction—does the speaker really believe this, or is he or she just saying it?

According to psychologist Albert Mehrabian, when listeners judge the emotional content of a speech, they give most weight to facial expression and body movement (55 percent). Vocal qualities count for 38 percent; the words themselves, only 7 percent.[34]

Importantly, the actions of your body will influence your

perception of your message! If you force yourself to smile and animate your body, you'll be much more likely to believe you're sharing a happy, interesting message than if you say the same words poker-faced.

When body, face, voice, and words are synchronized, your words are taken at face value. Body language then plays a supporting role—a critical role—but not the lead.

EYES

People who don't engage others with their eyes are judged less credible than those who do (unless they can't by virtue of blindness). This old saw has been played incessantly for decades, so there's no sense in belaboring it here. It's as near a truth like $2 \times 2 = 4$ as you'll ever get in the field of speech making.

But it's easier said than done. Looking at someone in conversation across a dinner table is child's play compared to looking at twenty-five people while projecting across a ten-foot channel of carpet or linoleum, all the while trying to decipher a script. Beginning and expert speakers alike have difficulty maintaining adequate eye contact with their listeners. As we noted in chapter 6, the cause of poor eye contact can often be traced to scripts of such poor legibility that the speaker dares not look up for fear of losing his place. And sometimes the cause is overconcern with the *words* of the presentation, rather than with the *ideas* the speaker wishes to communicate.

Assuming you have legible materials and the right attitude about your mission, how can the job of eye contact be made easier?

Put yourself at the podium and look up. What do you see? A happy face here . . . a sleepy face there . . . a bald guy in back leaving (for the rest room?) . . . a lady in a red blouse shuffling papers next to someone mopping a spilled cup of coffee . . . three guys in the middle who look like the Marx brothers. In brief, you see a lot. And that's the problem. You see too much.

Reducing the amount of visual stimulation is the first step to better eye contact. If our brains are consumed by the job of sorting out and making sense of all we see in the room before us, there isn't enough left to concentrate on what we have to say. To cope with the discomfort of seeing too much, many speakers will fix their gaze just over the heads of their listeners, talking to the air. The motivation behind this old technique is sound, but the result is not. People *can* tell that you're speaking to the exit door. The smaller the audience, the more obvious this ploy appears.

The answer to the dilemma—how to look at your audience without being visually overstimulated—is to look at and speak to one person at a time. Speak a complete idea to one person, then speak another idea to another person, and so on. Put into use, the method goes like this:

1. Look at your notes.
2. Absorb one idea.
3. Look up at one person and engage her eyes.
4. Speak your idea to that person (minimum five seconds).
5. Look down at your notes.
6. Absorb another idea.
7. Look up at another person and engage his eyes.

People who use this technique report a wonderful calming effect. They feel less strange. If you use it, it will be much easier to remember your material and your listeners will pay closer attention. A bonus effect occurs with a large group, say, over fifty. It will appear to the people sitting near your focus person that you are speaking to them directly.

About Glasses

Most near-sighted people need corrective lenses to deliver a speech well. But some people don't like to wear glasses; they believe wearing glasses makes them look old or infirm. A direct way around this problem is to use contact lenses. But for some, this is not an option.

If you must wear glasses, be sure they fit snugly. Buy those little antiskid pads for the nose bridge if your glasses are particularly heavy. Ill-fitting glasses will slip down your nose as you bend your head to see your notes. Your hand will naturally rise to push them up again just as you lift your head to reestablish eye contact. This can annoy an audience greatly. I vividly remember watching helplessly as the chief executive of a large bank virtually destroyed an otherwise good speech by engaging in a protracted battle to keep his reading glasses from falling to the podium. It is equally disconcerting to the listener when the speaker becomes wooden, fearing that any movement will send his loose glasses tumbling.

If you currently use bifocals or trifocals, consider substituting a pair of full-frame reading glasses for speech making. Speakers with half-frame reading glasses as well as those wearing old-style bifocals and trifocals appear to be looking down their noses at their listeners since they must elevate their chins to bring eyes, paper, and the reading segment of the lens, which is placed at the bottom, into alignment.

FACE

Few study faces more closely than actors—except perhaps negotiators and television producers. Roger Ailes is a former talk-show producer who got into communications consulting, eventually becoming then–Vice President George

Bush's media adviser during the 1988 presidential campaign. Ailes is widely credited with transforming George Bush's campaign image from a that of a sarcastic, "toothache of a man" into an upright, friendly person of strength and good will. How did this happen?

An examination of Bush's precampaign speeches with his memorable acceptance speech at the Republican national convention reveals a remarkable change in Bush's face. The smart-aleck grin is gone, replaced by a warm smile. The flying shocks of oiled hair are gone, replaced by a softer, but controlled style. The sporadic tosses of the head to one side are gone, replaced by gentler, more stable movements from side to side. The mouth that tended to force words out one side or the other is gone, replaced by a jaw moving up and down, rather than side to side. The transformation in personality wrought by these changes (and others, notably voice control) was remarkable. Out was the defensive swaggering and boyish gushing, in came the smooth confidence of deliberate, open expression.

The face is capable of a bewildering range of emotional expression—some say over seven thousand different expressions are possible from the eighty muscles of the face.[35] Unfortunately, without hard work and expert coaching, there is little most of us can do to significantly expand our range of expression. But we can work to eliminate distracting mannerisms if we know what they are.

The best way to ferret any kind of distracting physical behavior is to videotape one of your speech performances. For the purposes of the test, the more anxious you are, the better, because that's when your nervous tics will be most active. Turn off the sound and play the tape on fast forward. Any repetitive motion will become painfully obvious—from looking up at the ceiling to obsessive preening to swaying from side to side.

BODY

Purposeful Movement, Not Random

Next time you're at a pool, compare several swimmers doing the freestyle. What you'll discover, if you haven't already, is that what makes one swimmer better than another—in terms of both speed and endurance—is not body size, weight, or apparent muscularity. Apart from general conditioning, what makes one swimmer better than another is technique and control. Smoothness of stroke, coordination of breathing with arm extension, the general lack of random motion—these are the marks of a superior swimmer.

In good swimming, the expenditure of physical energy is regulated by the goal of propulsion. In good speaking, bodily movements are regulated by the goal of communication. Every movement—arm movements, shrugs, changes in stage location—should punctuate the message of the words, and not distract the audience from hearing their full meaning.

Your first objective is to reduce random movement. Nervous energy seems to leak out of speechmakers in similar ways—abrupt shifting of weight from one foot to another, frequent touching of face, pacing back and forth, and constant adjusting of clothing.

After gaining control over nervous movements, the next step is learning a wider range of *deliberate* physical expression. In other words, becoming more animated. This can mean taking acting lessons, or just observing and experimenting on your own.

The easiest and most natural way to become more animated and physically expressive is to be involved in what you're saying. Work at feeling the meaning of the words rather than just saying them. Permit yourself to get naturally excited about telling your story without fear of losing control.

The Basic Position

Jimmy Cagney once advised, "Walk in. Plant yourself. Look them in the eye and tell the truth." It's good advice. Every physical performance requires a basic position—a solid platform to support the movements your body must make to perform the task.

In stand-up speech making, the basic stance is this: feet twelve to eighteen inches apart, weight evenly distributed over the balls of both feet, body leaning slightly into the audience (never lean away), knees bent slightly, arms hanging freely at sides, hands out of pockets, elbows loose, not frozen.

Depart at will from the basic position to emphasize a point, acknowledge audience reaction, or gesture illustratively. And then return to the basic stance. Having a definite and familiar posture to return to will help boost your confidence to loosen up.

The basic position is more difficult to achieve than it appears to the audience. Stand up now and try it. Most people have a hard time standing still.

Small People with Big Podiums

Big podiums tend to swallow small people. If you're a small person confronted with a hulking podium, you have three choices:

1. Stand in front or to the side of the podium. Natasha Josefowitz, the slightly built author, poet, management consultant, and popular speaker, usually talks without notes in front of the podium.

2. Stand on a box behind the podium. Robert Reich, the compact author and economics professor at Harvard, once

came out on stage, mounted the little box in back of the podium, and said, "When I started teaching undergraduates at Harvard I was six feet tall."

3. Bring your own podium, built to your size. Michael Dukakis, the five-foot-ten-inch Democratic candidate for president, had a shorter podium than six-foot-four-inch Republican rival George Bush during their televised debates in the fall of 1988. Lee Iacocca, chairman of Chrysler, a man of regular build and a talented speaker, travelled with a specially made podium featuring push button controls for height adjustment, fan, microphone, and reading light!

Working the Frame

On the television screen, speakers are normally presented from the shoulders up. This is a narrow and highly focused frame of vision. Any gestures not within ten or so inches of the face will not be picked up by the camera. Slight facial gestures will be magnified by the close-up lens.

Contrast the speaker's image in this medium with that of a single speaker standing on a bare stage facing a room seating hundreds. The speaker on a large stage must work very hard indeed to dominate the audience's large field of vision, and make it visually interesting.

To work a large audience effectively, it is imperative to open up your posture. Widen your stance, loosen your joints, exaggerate every motion and gesture. For example, instead of merely shaking your head as a sign of disapproval, sweep your arm across your body and down at the same time. When working a small group, tighten up your gestures to avoid violating your listeners' personal space. The same goes when speaking to someone from across a desk, as in a job interview.

When speaking from behind a podium, keep all gestures above the waist or they won't be seen.

Stage Command

To be noticed and taken seriously, you must control a space and attract attention to it. And as we've noted, the larger the stage, the more animated the speaker must be. There's a fundamentalist preacher who, every Sunday morning, pulls a live audience numbering in the thousands and works them from a plain stage one hundred feet across. Of course, he might have less success if his subject wasn't the salvation of the soul, but trends in the tax-free bond market.

Outside the entertainment industry, only a handful of leaders need the ability to work a stage one hundred feet across. And many who do—captains of industry, most notably—have given up trying, resorting instead to large- and multiple-screen video displays.

Still, every speaker needs a modicum of stage command. In the absence of a master of ceremonies, the speaker is presumed in charge of the event. As Johnny Carson put it, "The only absolute rule is: Never lose control of the show." That's one reason for being animated.

The second reason is more self-serving—research has proven that a forward-leaning, engaged, fully animated person is much more credible than a retreating, disengaged, and rigid one.[36]

CLOTHING

Style

Outside of general good taste, on which sound advice abounds already, there is one important rule: The more controversial your ideas or affiliations, the more conventional your clothing should be. By conventional, I mean standard fare or a little better for the socio-economic group being addressed. There are exceptions, but since few speakers ever venture far from their own strata or culture to speak, there's no need to elaborate.

Contrast and Color

Against the greens and browns of natural foliage, any bird with red and yellow feathers will pop out from the background. The same principles apply to the plumage of speakers—if you want to be noticed, you must stand out from the background. This is done through movement and by attracting the audience visually to your face and upper body. A swatch of bright or contrasting color near the head and neck does this perfectly—hence the scarf, necktie, and pocket handkerchief industries.

Jewelry

Most jewelry interferes with speech making in one way or another. Necklaces are notorious for click-click-clicking through lapel microphones. Dangling bracelets can catch notes and hurl them across the stage. Generally, speech making and jewelry don't mix.

Dressing for Television

All earlier points apply plus a few others. Small patterns and checks wiggle and ghost the viewer's screen, so try not to wear them. Remove any piece of jewelry that will reflect the powerful studio lights into the camera—watches, earrings, rings. Remember that patent leather shoes and belt buckles also can blind the camera. Bright white blouses and stark white shirts should be avoided for the same reason. Furthermore, sharp contrasts between adjacent colors is as attracting to the eye as color itself. Humorously, media advisers during the 1988 elections seemed to have every male politician in the country wearing the same TV uniform—dark suit, blue shirt, reddish tie.

Comfort

Any piece of clothing that restricts your range of motion or constricts the cardiovascular system should be avoided. Tight belts and ties aggravate the shock phase of the alarm reaction.

Self-Image

Beyond the general rules, wear what makes you feel good.

VOICE

If the eyes are the windows of the soul, the voice is the front door. "There is no index of character as sure as the voice," said Benjamin Disraeli.

The elements of vocal quality are many. But most speech experts will say that the good speaker:

> is loud enough.
> has an adequate and varied rate of speech.
> uses clear diction.
> has a pleasant pitch.
> has good phrasing.
> uses frequent pauses.
> makes a variety of sound.

Loudness

It is abnormal to have an audience. We usually talk in small groups, with each person alternating speaking and listening. This is quite different from public speaking in two

ways. First, in casual conversation, speaking loudly is unnecessary and undesirable. Second, in casual conversation,
only raving boors will talk for five, ten, twenty, or thirty
minutes without stopping.

But this is what public speaking is all about—speaking
louder and a lot longer than normal. It is hard physical labor
for the oratorically flabby. Most people run out of air before
the end of their sentences because the sentences themselves
are too long and because more air is required to talk more
loudly.

To produce an adequate level of sound at a distance of,
say, twenty-five feet, more air under greater force must be
passed through the larynx, or voice box. To do this, you
must breathe and exhale smoothly and deeply. Standing or
sitting erect helps considerably, allowing the chest and ab-
domen to expand and contract freely. This is tough to do
if you don't believe it is all right for you to do it. So it's a
psychological as well as a physical challenge.

Muscles tight with nervous tension will impair your ability to speak loudly. Tight abdominal muscles will prevent
your lungs from expanding fully, thus reducing the volume
of air you have available just when you need it the most—at
the end of the sentence. Nervous tension also acts on the
throat, making the vocal cords taut. This results in higher
pitch than normal and occasionally cracking. The more nervous the speaker, the more difficult it will be to produce
adequate volume.

Rate

Unrelenting fast talkers can render an audience homicidal,
but slow talkers will make them suicidal. Either way, it's
murder.

Your listeners will appreciate it if you keep the ball rolling. Try to talk at a brisk, but pleasant rate. How fast is that?
In normal conversation, speakers can zip along at 200 to

300 words per minute. That's too fast for a speech. The most heavily coached speakers—presidents and presidential candidates—generally speak between 150 and 170 words a minute. The faster your rate, the clearer your diction must be.

Importantly, your rate of speech should match the emotional content. Sales pitches are usually given quickly in hopes of conveying a sense of excitement for the product. Eulogies and threats are delivered slowly, "in measured tones," indicating gravity. When the rate of speech does not match the content of the words spoken, the words are discounted. Try speaking the sentence "I am so excited" with a one-second pause between each word.

Finally, adrenaline has the effect of compressing time—it creates the illusion that time is passing very quickly, causing the beginning speaker to talk too fast. If this happens to you, write a big Slow Down sign on your notes. You can also place a confederate in the audience to cue you to speak faster or more slowly.

Diction

James Boren, a keen observer of white-collar behavior, once wrote a tongue-in-cheek bureaucratic code. Principle 1 was, "When in doubt, mumble." Boren's satiric comment reflected the truth that people who speak softly and with poor diction are regarded as less decisive, less intelligent, and more poorly informed than those who speak with round vowels and crisp consonants. Furthermore, good diction is an absolute must when speaking to the elderly, many of whom have great difficulty hearing consonants.

Pitch

A well-trained singer can produce two, three, and sometimes nearly four octaves of notes at will. But most people

have a speaking range of only one octave. This is acceptable
if many notes are used. Speakers who use only two or three
notes are boring—they drone.

Next to droning, the worst pitch-related problem is nasality. Think of whining three and four year olds. They have
the same effects on parents that whining speakers have on
audiences.

The last note on pitch is this: Try to end your sentences
on a low tone without dropping volume. If your pitch
goes up at the end of a sentence, you'll sound indecisive.
A sentence spoken with a rising pitch is almost universally
thought to be a question, not a statement. Speakers with
lower overall pitch and the pattern of dropping pitch (not
volume) at the ends of their phrases are perceived as more
credible than others who don't have these vocal qualities.

Phrasing and Pauses

A speaker with good phrasing speaks only one thought per
sentence . . . pauses . . . and says another. A longer sentence
is occasionally injected to add variety. By keeping sentences
short, the speaker is assured of getting enough air to produce them with adequate volume. Also, the listener's ear is
given a brief rest between thoughts, enabling better comprehension.

Beginning speakers are unfortunately reluctant to pause.
Many fear that if they stop producing words, even for a
second, they'll be unable to resume. Or they fear the attention that silence brings. These fears subside with experience. Soon the speaker learns the power of pausing; to
emphasize important points, to signal those critical transi-
tions between ideas, and to set up punch lines.

Speakers who phrase well and pause judiciously are universally regarded as more credible and knowledgeable than
those who dash straight to the end.

Variety

Listening is hard work. And, like any job, it is made easier
and more enjoyable by variation. Work hard to build in
changes of pace, a variety of sentence types (assertions,
questions, exclamations), changes in tone and loudness, as
well as variation in the length of your sentences. If you
sense that your audience is drifting away, you can easily
regain attention by changing volume, rate, or pitch.

9

BUILDING
ORATORICAL
POWER

Oratory has taken a bum rap lately, but this is hardly news. Eighteenth-century French historian Baron Montesquieu complained of the speakers of his day, saying, "What orators want in depth, they make up for in length."

Oratory is an old-fashioned word that just doesn't seem to cut it in an age preoccupied with facts. Ask someone to name an orator and odds are, they'll say, "Demosthenes— the guy who talked with rocks in his mouth," or "William Jennings Bryan—didn't he play opposite Spencer Tracy in *Inherit the Wind?*" Certainly, during every national election *The New York Times* will print an obligatory piece on oratorical technique, but that's about it.

Frankly, great skill in public speaking has always been more secretly feared than openly admired. Walter Cronkite—who, according to many polls taken during the 1970s and 1980s, was the most respected man in America—reflected on this after hearing one of Jesse Jackson's powerful campaign speeches. Cronkite said the anxiety many older voters felt over Jackson's candidacy was not, as might be first thought, due primarily to his race or political agenda.

Rather, Cronkite suspected that Jackson's ability to form an emotional bond with his impassioned followers revived frightening memories of the Axis demagogues of World War II.

Unfortunately, skillful use of the language in public is more often associated with deceit than with high purpose. This is primarily the fault of unscrupulous politicians who have labored long and low to cheapen the coin of rhetoric, the common-language twin of oratory. Reporters write of campaign speeches filled with "empty rhetoric," or worse. And usually it is worse. So much so that the word *rhetoric* has taken on an almost thoroughly negative connotation, being associated with clever distortions of fact, thinly veiled lies, and character assassination.

It may be temporarily impossible to rehabilitate rhetoric and oratory from the gutter of low repute, or elevate it from the cellar of history. But isn't it silly to think that skillful use of language should be avoided because some employ it to bad ends? Every speaker, ethical and otherwise, benefits from knowing and using legitimate rhetorical techniques, just as all speakers benefit from knowing how to start a speech or end one. But who would suggest to the speaker of good will that he or she deliberately start a speech poorly so as not to be thought a scoundrel?

It is a fact that the way words are chosen and assembled vastly influences the clarity and potency of the ideas they express. People the world over recall President John F. Kennedy's gift for inspiring, forceful, rhythmic speech. But as with most speakers, Kennedy's gift was no gift. It was a learned skill.

Kennedy's first speech to the Senate on May 18, 1953, was loaded with facts and specific proposals, the speech sounded very much like an economics lecture at the Harvard Business School. Kennedy spurned rhetoric and oratorical eloquence.

He did not bother with any stories, jokes, or even illustrative references for "human interest." He simply drove straight along his course.[37]

Rhetorical techniques can be divided into two principal categories: those to set the *tone* of the speech and those to increase the *effectiveness* of its contents by improving memorability or persuasiveness. Some of them do both and they tend to run in packs.

HOW TO AFFECT TONE

How do you want your words to sound? Like ball bearings bouncing in a brass bucket? As sweetbreads slipping into whipped cream? These are questions of tone, of how you want your words to *feel* when they hit the listener's eardrum.

1. For terse, gripping speech, use a series of short, declarative sentences. This is a useful technique for speeches to stimulate, as the following example shows:

> Now we're *told* all this is idealistic and weak. We can't afford compassion anymore. We have to be hard and macho. We have to electrocute more convicts. We have to support governments that torture their own people. We have to buy bigger weapons. And deny impoverished nations the help they need. We have to settle for less.
>
> —MARIO CUOMO, *governor of New York, speaking at Harvard, June 5, 1985.*[38]

2. For discursive speech, use longer sentences with clauses and asides. Casual speeches to inform as well as speeches to entertain are enhanced by this approach.

Soon I was sitting—yes, literally sitting—on a Persian rug in a little French summer house with Ibrahim Yazdi, one of those many "westernized" young Persians who was later to become one of Khomeini's revolving foreign ministers for five minutes. Now, ladies and gentlemen, I have always prided myself on being a rational woman, a realistic journalist, and I do not let my personal feelings get in the way of my professional behavior. Yet, when Khomeini came in, I had—to be truthful—the overwhelming feeling that I was in the presence of . . . consummate evil.

> —GEORGIE ANNE GEYER, *columnist and author, in a commencement address at St. Mary's College, May 14, 1988.* [39]

3. For punchy speech, use the harsh sounds of multiple consonants—*b*s, *k*s, hard *c*s, *p*s, and *r*s. Persuasive speeches often include sections with a punchy tone.

Revolution is never based on begging somebody for an integrated cup of coffee. Revolutions are never fought by turning the other cheek. Revolutions are never based upon love-your-enemy and pray-for-all-who-spitefully-use-you. And revolutions are never waged singing "We Shall Overcome." Revolutions are based upon bloodshed.

> —MALCOLM X, *in a speech called "The Black Revolution," delivered to a meeting sponsored by the Militant Labor Forum, New York City, 1960s.* [40]

4. For soothing speech, use soft consonants and full vowels. This technique is useful in stimulating feelings of security and comfort.

I may not be the most eloquent, but I learned early that eloquence won't draw oil from the ground. I may sometimes be a little awkward, but there's nothing self-conscious about my love of country. I am a quiet man, but I hear the quiet people others don't—the ones who raise the family, pay the taxes, meet the mortgage. I hear them and I am moved, and their concerns are mine.

> —VICE PRESIDENT GEORGE BUSH, *acceptance speech, Republican national convention, New Orleans, August 18, 1988.* [41]

5. For breezy speech, use contractions, slang, and fillers. This is a good way to ease into a serious topic without sounding overly grave.

> You know, tonight I feel a little like I did when I played basketball in the third grade. I thought I looked real cute in my uniform, and then I heard a boy yell from the bleachers, "Make that basket, bird legs."
> And my greatest fear is that same guy is somewhere out there in the audience tonight, and he's going to cut me down to size.
>
> —ANN RICHARDS, *in the keynote address to the Democratic national convention, July 18, 1988.* [42]

6. For formal, measured speech, lengthen sentences, do not use contractions, eliminate slang, opt for expressions with starch. Ceremonial speeches, including ribbon cuttings, formal announcements, eulogies, and award acceptance speeches, are naturals for this approach.

> I feel that this award was not made to me as a man, but to my work—a life's work in the agony and sweat of the human spirit, not for glory and least of all for profit, but to create out of the materials of the human spirit something which did not exist before.
>
> —WILLIAM FAULKNER *on accepting the 1949 Nobel Prize for Literature, Stockholm, Sweden, December 10, 1950.* [43]

Let every nation know, whether it wishes us well or ill, that we shall pay any price, bear any burden, meet any hardship, support any friend, oppose any foe to assure the survival and success of liberty.

> —PRESIDENT JOHN F. KENNEDY, *inaugural address, January 20, 1961.* [44]

NINE RHETORICAL TECHNIQUES
FOR MEMORABILITY
AND PERSUASIVENESS

1. Alliteration

Alliteration is a poetic device which works with any audience to ease the injection of notions not now in their noggins. It is the repetition of the same sound at the start of two or more words in the same phrase to create melody. However, in speech as in music, not all melodies please the ear. But that may well suit the speaker's purpose. The content of the words should always redeem the artifice of construction.

When Spiro Agnew, former vice president of the United States, complained about the "nattering nabobs of negativism," he used an alliteration concocted by one of his speechwriters, William Safire. When Reverend Jesse Jackson said at the 1984 Democratic national convention, "If in my low moments, in word, deed, or attitude, through some error of *temper, taste,* or *tone,* I have caused anyone discomfort, created pain, or revived someone's fears, that was not my truest self" he used alliteration (and tricolon, as described below).

2. Tricolon: The Rule of Three

Descriptive phrases, lists, and adjectives are more memorable when they travel in threes. The first two set the pace, the last brings them home.

> . . . that this nation, under God, shall have a new birth of freedom; and that government of the people, by the people, for the people shall not perish from this earth.

> —ABRAHAM LINCOLN, *address at Gettysburg, Nov. 19, 1863.* [45]

Our evidence is direct. It is precise. It is irrefutable.

> —PRESIDENT RONALD REAGAN *regarding Libyan Terrorism,*
> *April 14, 1986.*

So great is the ear's affection for triplets, that it altered Winston Churchill's most famous line. People remember Churchill as having said "blood, sweat, and tears." But he didn't. He actually said, "I have nothing to offer but blood, toil, tears, and sweat."

3. Ellipsis

Note above that Lincoln left out the *and* before the third phrase, "for the people." The technique is called *ellipsis,* omitting words to achieve speed and establish cadence.

> We must resist the temptation to train [students] only for an ever-longer list of specialties. We must teach reasons as well as answers . . . questions as well as techniques . . . values as well as methods.
>
> > —JOSEPH CURTIS, *on being installed chairman of the board of regents, Seattle University, September 25, 1981.*

4. Asyndeton

This odd word (pronounced eh-sin-deh-tun) refers to the use of sentence fragments to quicken the pace.

> The clear conception, outrunning the deductions of logic, the high purpose, the dauntless spirit, speaking on the tongue, beaming from the eye, informing every feature, and urging the whole man onward, right onward, to his object—this is eloquence, or rather it is something greater and higher than all eloquence—it is action, noble, sublime, godlike action.[46]

It is clear from the above example that the spoken word is governed by different rules of syntax than written language. What a speech looks like on paper is largely irrelevant to its value. What matters is how it sounds.

Asyndeton is often paired with ellipsis, as above. A more modern use of ellipsis turns a list into a trend.

> It took a century to develop photography . . . a half century to develop the telephone . . . a fifth of a century for commercial flight . . . a tenth of a century for television . . . a twentieth of a century to develop the atom bomb. The pattern is clear. The question is what next . . . and how soon?
>
> —FRANK G. WELLS, *president of the Disney Company, in a speech to the annual convention of the American Travel Industry Association, October 29, 1987.* [47]

5. Anaphora

Anaphora is the grand dame of political rhetoric. Successive sentences are begun with the same word or group of words. The effect is as familiar as the classic example:

> We shall fight in France, we shall fight on the seas and oceans, we shall fight with growing confidence and growing strength in the air, we shall defend our island, whatever the cost may be, we shall fight on the beaches, we shall fight on the land grounds, we shall fight in the fields and in the streets, we shall fight in the hills; we shall never surrender.
>
> —WINSTON CHURCHILL *to the House of Commons, June 4, 1940.*

Though often running as a racehorse for politicians, anaphora is also a sturdy workhorse, easily harnessed to the purpose of commerce.

It doesn't matter if we can communicate faster and cheaper than ever before—if we keep on communicating the same old message. It doesn't matter if we can design and plan by computer—if it allows us to make the same mistakes more quickly. It doesn't matter if technology can provide us new products and services—if we can't apply them to our needs.

> —ROBERT ANDERSON, *chairman, Rockwell International, in a speech to the Cal Tech Executive Forum in 1982.*

6. Balance

A balanced phrase opposes two elements, the first usually spoken with pitch going up, the second with pitch going down. It is effective in moderation only. Using it too often produces a sing-song effect.

> I look forward to a great future for America—a future in which our country will match its military strength with our moral restraint, its wealth with our wisdom, its power with our purpose.
>
> —JOHN F. KENNEDY, *Amherst College, October 26, 1963.*

Extremism in the defense of liberty is no vice. Moderation in the pursuit of justice is no virtue.

> —SENATOR BARRY GOLDWATER, *1964 presidential campaign.*

Conquer, or die.

> —HANNIBAL *to his troops, 218* B.C.

After all is said and done, more is said than done.

> —ANONYMOUS

7. The Rhetorical Question

Questions serve many purposes in speech. Common parlance calls them rhetorical when they are used primarily for effect.

To Issue a Challenge

> Where is the economic recovery for those who are sleeping in the snow and the cold of our streets?
>
> —SENATOR EDWARD M. KENNEDY, *at the Alf Landon lecture series, Manhattan, Kansas, January 30, 1984.*

To Introduce an Idea for Discussion

The speaker asks a question only as a pretext for answering it. Very handy for moving a speech along.

> Why did a speech at a small Midwestern college by a seventy-two-year-old former British prime minister who had been overwhelmingly defeated at the polls just six months before have such an impact?
>
> —FORMER PRESIDENT RICHARD NIXON *(referring to Winston Churchill's "Iron Curtain" speech given at Westminster College in Fulton, Missouri, in 1946), to the Los Angeles World Affairs Council, March 6, 1986.*

To Indicate Misunderstanding, Real or Feigned

A speaker may ask a question in such a way as to imply that any answer to it is either trivial or misguided.

> How is Moscow threatened if the capitals of other nations are protected? We do not ask the Soviet leaders—whose country has suffered so much from war—to leave their people de-

fenseless against foreign attack. Why then do they insist that we
remain undefended?

> —PRESIDENT RONALD REAGAN, *for the fortieth anniversary of
> the United Nations, October 24, 1985.* [48]

To Make an Accusation or Introduce an Idea as Fact

When, O Cataline, do you mean to cease abusing our pa-
tience? How long is that madness of yours to mock us? When
is there to be an end of that unbridled audacity of yours,
swaggering about as it does now?

> —CICERO, *One of the greatest orators of any age,* 63 B.C.

This technique is used fairly when evidence abounds that
the assumption is true; unfairly when the questioner has
little or no evidence, seeking to injure by implication.
Hence the classic, When did you stop beating your wife?

8. Hyperbole

An exaggeration used to emphasize a point, though not
prove it, is called hyperbole. There are mild exaggerations
and there are whoppers. There are exaggerations to increase the value of something, and those to denigrate it. But
remember that when a person is denigrated through hyperbole, it can be construed as character assassination. There
are also exaggerations to make something seem more urgent, or less so.

> Those "just say no" [to sex] messages are about as effective
> at preventing [teen] pregnancy as saying "have a nice day"
> prevents chronic depression.

> —FAYE WATTLETON, *president of Planned Parenthood Federation
> of America, in a speech in Seattle, October 21, 1988.* [49]

The world's best hopes lie with America's future.

> —PRESIDENT RONALD REAGAN, *State of the Union Address 1986.*

Eighty percent of success is showing up.

> —WOODY ALLEN, *Comic.*

Our stock is going down like Niagara Falls.

> —WILLIAM M. JENKINS, *former chairman, Seafirst Corporation, 1982.*

As a colleague of mine remarked the other day, predicting the course of events is like trying to tattoo a soap bubble.

> —CLIFTON GARVIN, JR., *chairman, Exxon Corporation, at the Economic Club of Detroit, April 26, 1982.*

My opponent has been against just about every new weapons system since the slingshot.

> —VICE PRESIDENT GEORGE BUSH, *speaking against opponent Michael Dukakis during the 1988 presidential election campaign.*

One-fifth of the people are against everything all the time.

> —ROBERT F. KENNEDY.

If you stay in Beverly Hills too long, you become a Mercedes.

> —ROBERT REDFORD, *actor.*

The thrift industry is really in terrible shape. It's reached the point where if you buy a toaster, you get a free savings and loan.

> —SENATOR LLOYD BENTSEN, *January 28, 1989.*

9. Repetition

A thematic phrase or word is repeated throughout a passage or, for that matter, the entire speech. Repetition is the oldest device known for getting something into memory. It has the effect of unifying long blocks of spoken words. The chosen phrase itself serves as a focal point for the audience's approval and, if appropriate, applause.

Most poor people are not on welfare. They work every day. They take the early bus. They work every day.

They care for other people's babies and they can't watch their own. They cook other people's food and carry leftovers home. They work every day.

They are janitors running the buffing machines. They are nurses and orderlies wiping the bodies of the sick. A loaf of bread is no cheaper for them than it is for the doctor. They work every day.

They put on uniforms and are considered less than a person. They change beds in the hotels. Sweep our streets. Clean the schools for our children. They're called lazy, but they work every day. They work in hospitals. They mop the floors. They clean the commodes, the bedpans. They work every day. No job is beneath them. And yet when they get sick, they cannot afford to lie in the bed they've made up every day.

—*The* REVEREND JESSE JACKSON, *campaigning for the Presidency in California, May 1988.* [50]

Part Three

TOPICS OF SPECIAL INTEREST

10

THE ELEMENTS OF PERSUASION

Nearly every day for nineteen consecutive sessions of the United States Senate, William Proxmire of Wisconsin rose to speak in support of a single bill—a bill introduced in 1949. In all, Proxmire delivered more than 3,300 speeches to the Senate on behalf of the measure now known as the Proxmire Act, which was finally passed on February 11, 1986. Two years later, the House of Representatives sent it to the president, who signed it into law.

What was this bill, this proposal so controversial that it took forty years for a majority of the Senate to approve it? The answer is more astounding than Proxmire's persistence. The bill makes genocide—the deliberate destruction of a specific population—illegal under U.S. law and sets penalties for violators. That's all. I doubt you could find 1,000 people in the 250-million-strong United States who believe it shouldn't be illegal to annihilate whole races of people. Yet it took over forty years and 3,300 speeches to get a prohibition through the Senate.

Inside the individual, as well as inside the group, there are competing and conflicting beliefs and values. Getting something through the morass can be a very complex undertaking.

But it can be done, and many things make it easier. The purpose of this chapter is to give you, in one place, a summary of significant findings on persuasion. Not all of them, of course. Only those relating to the aims of public speakers.

Luckily or unluckily, we've never lacked for experts on persuasion. They hail from three fields of study—philosophy, political theory, and psychology—and each discipline has produced important insights into the persuasive process.

PHILOSOPHERS ON PERSUASION

Learning to reason is a process that begins at birth. And so it is fitting that reasoning would be the first subject studied in depth by Greek philosophers at the birth of Western civilization. The great philosophers—Socrates, Plato, and Aristotle—sought a science of reasoning. Their passion: to make objective inquiry possible by discovering the principles of inductive and deductive reasoning. These philosophers assumed that once the laws of thought were discovered, people would work cooperatively to discover great truths—or at least reach the same conclusions from the same facts.

But more than logic is needed to persuade. If we followed the course laid by the great philosophers, we would have to conclude that persuading people is simply a matter of establishing facts and walking together down the steps of a rational calculus.

But we've all seen there's more to it than this. The flame of rational consistency often burns faintly in the human breast. Most religions, for example, *teach* the inapplicability of reason to matters of faith. And many nonreligious beliefs are often held as articles of faith—even by paragons of clear thinking. Former President Dwight Eisenhower firmly believed that Swedish socialism was a major cause of suicide in that country. Religion, addiction, habit, pet theories, prejudice—all these and more prevent people from being persuaded by facts alone.

Then again, one person's fact can be another's mirage. The history of science abounds with examples of eminent scientists unmoved by forceful arguments, choosing traditional thinking over evidence. For fifteen hundred years, scientists believed that arrows shot through the air remained in flight not from inertia, but from the pressure of air moving in behind to fill the "vacuum" created by the arrow's forward movement. Why did they believe this? Because Aristotle said it was so.

So logic is not everything. But it remains an important element in the persuader's repertoire. It's a fact verifiable from our own experience that speakers who present sound arguments and well-reasoned opinions are more convincing than those who do not.[51]

POLITICIANS ON PERSUASION

Early political theorists discovered that reputation and appearances are vital ingredients in the persuasive stew. The most famous of these thinkers were two advisors to the sixteenth-century Italian court—Niccolò Machiavelli and Conte Baldassare Castiglione.

Obsessed with power—how to get it and how to keep it—Machiavelli wrote *The Prince* to advise potential rulers on how to persuade the fractious Italians to obey them. For Machiavelli, the essence of persuasiveness was looking and acting the part of a person deserving of power. Machiavelli's great insight is that powerful people must appear able to bear the cost of impeccably virtuous behavior. On public speaking, Machiavelli is best remembered for saying:

> A prince [one aspiring to leadership] must take great care that nothing goes out of his mouth which is not full of these five qualities: Mercy, Faith, Integrity, Humanity, and Religion.

Like Machiavelli, Castiglione was a "flak," an advisor in the Italian court; he died in 1529 after a brief career as a writer and diplomat. Like Machiavelli, Castiglione believed that speech was critical to power. In his book *Il Cortegiano* (The Courtier), Castiglione says:

> Particularly valuable in impressing people is the art of conversation. Whenever possible, [the courtier] should prepare himself in advance while pretending to do the whole thing extempore.

Today, the occupational descendants of Machiavelli and Castiglione include legions of media consultants, handlers, image advisors, pollsters, spin doctors, and charisma consultants who direct the campaigns of major political candidates. Image consultants are available to the masses, too. Dale Carnegie's *How To Win Friends and Influence People,* Michael Korda's *Power, How To Get it and How To Use It,* and John T. Malloy's *Dress for Success* are three of the twentieth century's best selling how-to books, all devoted to the development and maintenance of the persuasive persona.

PSYCHOLOGISTS ON PERSUASION

Experiments by social and clinical psychologists have told us a great deal about attitude formation and cognitive development. The bad news is that psychological research has confirmed what we already know: People are stubborn and egocentric, strongly committed to their own point of view—no matter how wrongheaded that might appear. Two researchers present their painfully forthright synopsis of this fact as follows:

> . . . the main lesson to be drawn from our study is how very resistant people are to messages that fail to fit into their own picture of the world and their own objective circumstances, [and] how they deliberately (if unconsciously) seek out only those views which agree with their own.[52]

While psychological research has done much more than tell us what we already know, there have been no big surprises. Which is good. If psychologists revealed that we don't operate *at all* as we appear to ourselves and others, something would be very wrong about psychology. But psychologists *have* shed uncommon clarity on *how* people judge public speakers and evaluate what they have to say. Beginning with experiments on attitude change done at Yale University in the 1950s, psychological research has shown that the elements of persuasion are threefold:

Source Credibility.
Effective Argumentation.
Body Language.

Thanks to psychological research, we know with a high degree of confidence what leads people to judge a speaker credible or incredible. We know why some ways of arguing are more effective than others. We also know what kind of body language will enhance a speaker's credibility and what kind will detract.

THE PRAGMATICS OF PERSUASION

With a deep bow to every source, here's just about all I know and consider worth telling about persuasive speaking.

Source Credibility

Reputation

Incoming Boeing Company president Frank Shrontz gave a speech in 1985 to officials of the U.S. government's Air Force Systems Command—a major buyer of Boeing products. He said,

> We—and I mean both our industry in general and my company in particular—have done some dumb things. I think we must admit that waste, fraud, and abuse do exist. You know it, and I know it. No system this large and complex is without flaws. But I think it would be a lot more effective for us to stop trying to claim we're perfect or poor victims of the press.[53]

Why would Shrontz say such negative things about his company? Because a few weeks earlier his employer made national headlines for overcharging the government hundreds of dollars for a simple pair of pliers, hundreds more for a few plastic, no-skid caps for the legs of a stool. When the facts first came to light amid a general investigation into defense industry fraud, another Boeing official defended Boeing's bills. This official insisted the billings were proper, saying the pliers and plastic caps required expensive tooling. His explanation didn't wash in the press. In a matter of weeks, Boeing's reputation, built on decades of reliable, breakthrough products in aviation, aerospace, and avionics, was headed straight into the ground. Shrontz's blunt admission and acceptance of blame was a rare, but also necessary, move—not only for Boeing, but for Shrontz's personal reputation as well. Had Shrontz not moved immediately to overcome his guilt-by-association with the previous company line, many of his later statements would have been met with greater skepticism.

A deserved reputation for honesty is your most persuasive point.

Your Introduction

When you are not well known to the audience—and even when you are—someone is normally given the job of introducing you, of establishing or confirming your reputation. This ritualistic act is critically important. A good introduction can boost you considerably; bad ones drain your energy and the audience's respect. Many platform speakers write out a suggested script of introduction to avoid the embarrassment of an inaccurate, demeaning, overly long, or frivolous introduction.

Belief and Attitude Similarity

"Does this guy share my slant on life?" That's what your listeners want to know. Studies have shown that when you introduce a controversial idea, you will be more persuasive if you clearly mention other points on which you agree with your listeners—even if these points are completely unrelated to the topic at hand.[54] This is the wisdom behind the common-bond technique for opening a speech described in chapter 4.

President Gerald Ford was debating Georgia Governor Jimmy Carter during the 1976 presidential campaign when he boldly asserted that Poland was not under the political control of the Soviet Union. To some, Ford's statement was just a lapse or piece of harmless bravado. But most people were shocked at Ford's lack of knowledge. In any case, they felt it was insensitive to the Polish people. Ford's ratings in the polls plummeted because he failed to publicly correct his error, choosing rather to defend it weakly or avoid it. His candidacy never recovered.

Occasionally, a single belief or value can be a litmus test for your acceptance. If so, when you are in agreement, you'll benefit from saying so early in the speech. If you disagree, you should avoid the issue completely. It's important to remember that even when you stand apart from the audience on some issues, there is usually considerable acreage of common ground remaining. The more antagonistic the group, the more vigorously you need to assert your allegiance to that common ground—whatever it is.

Control over Environment

In earlier chapters we saw the importance of stage presence and control over props and other visual devices, as well as the importance of smooth staging and event coordination. Microphones that squeak, slides that pop up out of order, notes that fall off the lectern—all these detract from a speaker's overall credibility. Needless to say, the credibility of anyone involved in a product demonstration is directly tied to how well the product performs in the demonstration.

Your Appearance

1. People tend to like and believe people who look, dress, and act like themselves over those who do not.

2. If the speaker wears a uniform, it helps or hinders according to the reputation of the issuing agency.

3. The importance of appearance is inversely proportionate to the length of the speaker-audience encounter; that is, the less time you have, the more important your appearance figures into your credibility. The more time you have, the more other factors come into play, while the importance of appearance diminishes.

Fairness

How fairly do you approach the argument? Your character will be damaged if the audience detects a purposeful misrepresentation of fact. Also, if you cavalierly reject an opposing view with innuendo and hyperbole, it might play well to a partisan audience. But it won't play at all well with an undecided audience. And an opposing audience will go nuts.

Do you overstate problems, exaggerate benefits, underestimate disadvantages? Fairness cues can be subtle to the speaker, but critical listeners pick them up like money on the sidewalk—with a gleeful gotcha. A land developer seeking community approval for a neighborhood convenience store came to a meeting of concerned citizens. He loudly asserted that the neighbors need not worry because the store would be "owner-operated." This conjured images of ma and pop running the corner market. Under relentless questioning, the developer clarified his terms— the "owner" to whom he referred would be the multitudes of stockholders of a thousand-store chain. They would legally "operate" the store through an elected board of directors. These directors would "operate" the store from the out-of-state corporate headquarters office by hiring local people at minimum wages to keep the facility open twenty-four hours a day. Therefore, he said, the store would be owner-operated. His presentation went downhill from there.

EFFECTIVE ARGUMENTATION

Why are some speakers convincing and others not? Credibility is one factor, and as we shall note shortly, so is style of delivery. The third factor is content. *What* is said and *how* it is said must be considered carefully by the speaker bent on persuasion.

Unfortunately, few principles of effective argumentation work consistently well. Too much depends on the circumstances of the moment. It would be foolish to tell the chess player, "When you want to win at chess, play pawn to rook 4, sacrifice your bishops, and lead with your queen." For many of the same reasons it would be foolish to advise the speaker, "When you want to be persuasive, use indirect proof, lots of allusions to the Bible, and that story about Charles de Gaulle."

Knowing how to express a point of view so that a particular group of listeners will be moved to accept it is a skill acquired gradually, throughout a lifetime. Jill Ruckelshaus has noted that "the best way to win an argument is to begin by being right." Beyond this, there are basic moves and advanced moves. People get better at using them with practice. At first it seems almost unethical to consciously use a persuasive pattern of speech. After a while, though, your ethical code will learn to distinguish fair from unfair argument.

Rational and Emotional Appeals

A speaker can make an idea more believable by supporting it with either rational appeals or emotional appeals—or both.

Rational Appeals

Examples. Statistics. Expert testimony. Illustrations. These are the most common and versatile kinds of rational appeals. A speaker using them is saying, "You should believe this because the experts say it's true, experience confirms it, the numbers back it up, and it's easy to see how it works." We discussed in chapter 4 how to most effectively use various kinds of rational support.

Rational appeals are expected to be predominant in most management settings. In sales, as we'll see, emotional appeals are more common. Generally, rational appeals are most persuasive to listeners who haven't much to lose or gain from either side of your proposal. Such appeals also work to reinforce the convictions of the already converted.

But, as we've already seen, rational support doesn't carry much weight when the listener is controlled by powerful emotions. Representatives of the nuclear power industry in the mid-1980s were shocked to learn that their efforts to calm public unrest over nuclear plant safety had just the opposite effect. Their educational campaign to bury myths about nuclear power by showing how reactors really worked backfired in an unexpected way: Once people learned how the safety systems at the plants were engineered, it was easier for them to imagine how they could fail. To the unscientific, a one-in-six-million chance of something going wrong is not much different from a one-in-six hundred chance. Psychologists tell us that the ability to picture something in detail makes it seem more real—or more likely to occur.[55]

Another example of the irrationality of men and women comes to us from the Congress of the United States. Representatives hearing testimony by Environmental Protection Agency officials to support the miles-per-gallon ratings given to various autos have been known to reject the EPA's

findings (based on a sample size of ten or more cars) if a
fellow representative reports a different result with his or
her own car. In these cases, highly biased, anecdotal evidence is taken as more authoritative than a scientifically
controlled test.

What can you do? When your listeners just don't think
straight, there's not much you *can* do to straighten them
out—certainly not in a few minutes.

Emotional Appeals

Speakers are far more likely to encounter listeners ruled by
a complex interplay of emotion and logic than by logic
alone. Thus, it is best to appeal to the listener's heart as well
as to his head. Of course, when listeners are overcome by
strong emotions—and these can be anywhere along Maslow's hierarchy of needs (described in chapter 5)—rational
argument by itself is inappropriate as well as useless.

Political and religious leaders, who deal with emotional
subjects on a full-time basis, know that once an audience is
in an emotionally aroused state, nearly any emotion present
in the listener can be easily called up just by naming it and
talking about it. Once this has been done, the speaker simply associates his or her proposals with the unleashed emotional bulldozer, sits back, and watches the walls of resistance crumble. The listener's conviction for the proposal
will be directly proportional to the strength of the emotions associated with it. Here are some common emotions
to which speakers often appeal to support their ideas.

Justice and Fair Play:

I believe that fair-minded people will give Blemis Chemical its
day in court. They may not want to, but they know justice
requires it.

Patriotism:

If you love your country as I do . . . if you believe in what it stands for . . . if you'll stand up for it, then your love of country will tell you to stand with me and support the president's initiative.

Greed:

Have you ever wondered what it would be like to have so much money that you couldn't count it all? So much money that could buy anything—*anything*—that you wanted? You can have that kind of money if you subscribe now.

Feelings of Sympathy for Others:

Doesn't your heart go out to baby Jessica? If you'd like to help . . .

Desire for Freedom:

When you're a member of Lincoln Health Plans, you're free to choose your own physician from among hundreds of board-certified doctors. And should you at anytime become dissatisfied, you can change. Isn't this better than being locked into a choice that wasn't your own?

Guilt or Shame:

How will you feel tomorrow when you wake up and find your car has been repossessed? Send us the money and avoid the embarrassment.

Conformity:

Sacred Harmony is where most parents in Broadmire send their children. We hope your daughter will join us too.

Fear:

You'll rest easy at night with the Ersatz Security System guarding your life and property.

Most speakers instinctively realize there are ethical issues involved in motivating people through emotional appeals. Appeals to greed are almost universally rejected as unethical. And it's wrong to play on people's fears when there is no danger or when the proposal will not make them safer or happier. It is also wrong to plant worries which are not there. One of my teachers, Jerry Tarver of the University of Richmond, gave the example of an encyclopedia sales boss who suggested this unethical pitch: "If you don't want your child to be retarded, you'd better have a set of these around the house to stimulate his intelligence."

But how about appeals to sympathy, patriotism, the desire for freedom, or a sense of fair play? Very often, one of these high- or middle-ground emotional appeals will be just what you need to win the listener over.

Ten Thoughts on Effective Argumentation

1. People are more averse to loss than motivated by gain. An example comes from the credit-card industry. When credit-card interest rates were high in the early 1980s, some merchants wanted to give customers an incentive to pay with cash. The credit-card industry vigorously lobbied the major retail chains to call their incentive a "discount for cash" instead of a "credit surcharge." They knew that more customers would give up a discount for cash (forgo a gain by using the card) than would pay a surcharge (suffer a loss by using the card).[56]

Mobile carpet cleaners often use this principle of loss avoidance in their pitch for a soil-retardant chemical spray which is sold and billed separately from the cleaning itself. Here's how it works. After the carpet has been cleaned, the customer is approached and told that the carpet will stay clean with the spray for far longer than it would without it. The homeowner really doesn't know if the spray will work, but wants to avoid losing his now-clean carpet. This works to the carpet cleaner's favor.

2. Avoid stiffening resistance—reframe the issue or use indirect proof. As we saw in Chapter 4 when discussing ways to organize a persuasive speech, one way to avoid coming to an impasse with an opponent is to reframe the issue. That is, recast the problem in terms of the listeners' desires. For example, telling adolescents they shouldn't smoke because smoking leads to heart disease is not persuasive. Teenagers have always known they are immortal. It is more effective to note the teenagers' need for acceptance and love and note that people who do not smoke are more attractive than those who do.

We also saw the usefulness of inductive argument in which the speaker totes up evidence gradually, casually, until drawing the inevitable conclusion.

Also, avoid stiffening resistance by refraining from the use of inflammatory language. People are likely to become *more* attached to their ideas if they are called stupid or their plans are dubbed idiotic, scurrilous, lame, preposterous, and dumb.

3. Remember to reinforce the link between support and the idea supported. Unless you remind them, your listeners are apt to forget the point that your evidence was trotted out to prove. This is true particularly in the middle of the speech—the place where most of your evidence will be. Get into the habit of saying things like, "So you see, the report of Consumers Union as well as the testimony of thousands of happy campers proves it—the Denali bag is a must item for the well-stocked outdoor retailer."

4. A variety of support is more convincing than one kind only.

5. Good argumentation observes protocol. For example, if you're trying to convince the town council to convert an

old school building into housing for the elderly, you'll do well to argue that the benefits of your proposal are greater—and the disadvantages smaller—than those of competing options. The reason: because this pattern of presentation matches the decision-making process of the legislative body, which is to deliberate, to weigh options. Because your *style* of argumentation fits, your arguments themselves will have more force, appear more credible.

6. Effective argumentation depends on the balance of power between persuader and listener. A parent can convince a child to eat his peas by *threatening* to withhold dessert—sometimes!—because the parent has the power to do it. On the other end, the child will try to *cajole* and *wheedle* out of pea-eating—because the child can't do what he or she wants without parental approval. Submission, however, is a fragile and dubious form of persuasion.

7. Generating cognitive dissonance *can* be effective. The theory of cognitive dissonance comes from psychologist Leon Festinger.[57] He said in 1957 that any particular belief a person has will either be consonant with his other beliefs, dissonant, or irrelevant. When a person becomes aware that two of his beliefs are dissonant (contradictory), the person will search for a way to reject one of the beliefs rather than endure the emotional discomfort of holding contradictory views.

For example, the king's valet has always despised the king. Then, years after the king has died, the valet discovers that it was the king who had anonymously paid for his son's education. The valet has a choice: devalue his son's education or feel more kindly about the departed king. Which will it be? In time, other ways of dealing with the dilemma will present themselves. (Probably through years of therapy!)

The idea that people must act to reduce cognitive dissonance opens new avenues of persuasion for canny persuaders. For example, the speaker points to two or more beliefs held strongly by the listener and notes that these beliefs can't all be true. Then the speaker's thesis is offered as a way to eliminate the conflict between the ideas, making them consonant once more.

Public relations experts called in to improve the image of publicly embattled corporations usually recommend that the corporation immediately boost its support for worthy causes. Then the public must decide—either the cause isn't worthy or the company isn't so bad after all (or the company is still bad, just trying to buy virtue).

Because cognitive dissonance makes the listener uncomfortable, the speaker who generates it may appear presumptuous, and lose in personal popularity what little is gained in persuasiveness.

8. Anticipate immediate objections and defend against ones they'll hear later. This is sometimes called balancing. Research indicates that listeners are less likely to accept an argument at face value if they've already heard it voluntarily brought up and refuted by a credible speaker.

9. Persistence pays.

Press on. Nothing in the world can take the place of persistence. Talent will not; as nothing is more common than unsuccessful individuals with talent. Genius will not; unrewarded genius is almost a proverb. Education will not; the world is full of overeducated derelicts. Persistence and determination alone seem always to prevail.

—RAY KROC, *founder of McDonald's restaurants, the largest restaurant chain in the world.* [58]

10. Give your best support first; your next-best last. Psychologists tell us that listeners give more weight to, and are better able to remember, the first and last things

they hear. This is called the primacy and recency effect. The effect is important in persuasive writing, but even more so in speech because the listeners cannot, as we've noted before, go back at their leisure and review the speaker's every word; their reflections are limited by the quirks of memory.

For the same reason, in a series of speakers, the first and last slots are best.

PERSUASIVE BODY LANGUAGE

Don't be excessively concerned if your podium presence is a *little* stiff. There's good evidence that clarity and substance, content and organization can outweigh delivery skill in the persuasive balance.[59]

But as we noted in chapter 8, if your words say "trust me," while your body says "boorish tyrant" or "indecisive nebbish," your body will do the talking. We have it on good authority that relaxed and purposeful body movement and voice control will greatly enhance your credibility *and* increase the perceived importance of your ideas.

Professors Roger Masters and Denis Sullivan of Dartmouth College have gone so far as to say that speaking style (particularly facial expressions), rather than content or organization, made the difference in three recent presidential elections. Masters studied the videotapes of the presidential election debates in 1960, 1976, and 1980. He found striking similarities among the speaking styles of the winners—and among the losers. In 1960, the relaxed, good-humored John Kennedy beat the stiff, strident, aggressive Richard Nixon. In 1976, the smiling, humble, calm demeanor of

Jimmy Carter beat the nervous, fumbling, serious Gerald Ford. And in 1980, the good-natured, homespun Ronald Reagan outdistanced the angry, argumentative, and obsessed Jimmy Carter.

Masters and Sullivan contend that our reactions to different facial expressions are instinctual: "For five million years people have been depending on these animal cues to see whether that individual in front of them is going to bite them or not."[60]

Reporters following Senator Gary Hart during his 1984 bid for the Democratic Party's presidential nomination criticized Hart's mid-campaign delivery style, saying Hart's glaring eyes and knitted eyebrows "gave an impression of overconcern." Soon, Hart was seen joking more, trying to soften his strident message. Hart's new demeanor during this period was not limited to the podium. Some remember the senator surfing down the aisle of a Boeing 757 during takeoff atop two emergency instruction cards.

Certainly, factors *other than* body language affect the outcomes of persuasive contests. Still, the observation that a confident, good-natured presence is important to persuasion has been supported by other communications researchers, most notably that cited by Nancy Henley in her landmark *Body Language,* and by Zimbardo, Ebbesen, and Maslach in their book, *Influencing Attitudes and Changing Behavior.*

Grossly simplified, the research shows that if you do the following things, you'll be more persuasive than if you don't.

- Face your listeners as much as possible.
- Hold eye contact at least 50 percent of the time you talk.
- Make your facial expression match your ideas and emotions.
- Move on purpose, not skittishly.
- Speak in a natural voice, but without nasality.

- Maintain a forward-leaning posture, engage the listener.
- Wear conservative clothing for unconventional ideas.
- Relax your face and jaw.
- Vary your speaking rate to hold interest.
- Avoid strident, insistent tones—unless danger exists.
- Speak up so people can hear you.

11

Humor

If you're tired of writers who turn pasty at the thought of "dissecting" humor, this chapter's for you. You know the writers I mean—whimpering around the keyboard, moaning that we can't reveal the inner workings of humor without killing it. (As if they'd be the first to slaughter a joke.) Still, they complain, humor is too precious a thing. Blah blah blah.

There was a story in the paper a while ago about a little girl who refused to dissect a frog in her biology class because she was morally opposed to wanton frog killing. Her teacher graded her down anyway so the girl took it all the way to the Supreme Court. The Supreme Court said the school could make her do it—but only if they gave her frogs already dead from natural causes. Natural causes. Can you imagine anything more pitiful than a bunch of old frogs floating around the pond waiting to die?

Neither can I. I say this: If our choice is between advancing human understanding by swiftly and mercifully ending the life of some old jokes, or callously watching them waste away, alone and unappreciated in some third-rate toad house, I say, "Let's be strong. Let the carnage begin."

FIRST CONSIDERATIONS

Speakers vs. Comedians, Humor vs. Jokes

When you're only after laughs, you're more comedian than speechmaker. And for a comedian, the number and loudness of laughs is the best, and perhaps the only, gauge of success. Comics working the borscht belt of family vacation spots in the Catskill and Pocono mountains after World War II had a name for it—they called it a "tummel," which, loosly translated, means "a ruckus." You have a tummel when most of the audience is laughing constantly, only stopping for air. They're not so broken up that they're gasping, but a rolling, continuous state of mirth has consumed them. Everything you say just makes them laugh more. Once an audience is in the grips of a tummel, the lore goes, you can throw them anything and they'll love it.

Stand-up comedy is a venerable profession, but the speech to inform or persuade is no place to practice. Usually all you'll want or need for pep is an occasional chuckle or a nodding smile of recognition. Rarely will you want or need belly laughs. They take too long, for one thing.

Television comedy also sets inappropriate standards for planning and judging speech humor. A good monologue for a television comic is expected to pull a laugh every twenty seconds—and that's the minimum. Danny Simon, a veteran television comedy writer who began writing for Sid Caesar's "Show of Shows" in the 1950s, laments that screenwriters for today's situation comedies are issued laugh-line quotas for every scene and every period between commercials.

But in speeches, humor is not an end, only a pleasant way to achieve other goals. Even the after-dinner speech to entertain has a theme, a moral, or a principle.

Both speaker and comedian may be humorists, but the speaker must understand humor in a broader context. Humor in speeches should have the feel of truth, not contrivance. The best humor for speeches is fresh from life, from yours or someone else's—perhaps a funny thing you read that illustrates your point, or a witticism from a famous person that you can use to introduce or summarize a point. The most important thing here is that whatever humor you use, it should increase—not decrease—the authenticity of your ideas.

What Humor Can Do for and to a Speech

1. Reveal important truths.
2. Increase your likability and persuasiveness.
3. Move your ideas forward.
4. Alter your pace and tone.
5. Boost your confidence.
6. Bring needed merriment to all.

But humor badly done can have exactly the opposite effects. It can mangle the truth. It can make an audience detest you. It can stop your ideas cold. It can reinforce the current mood. It can make you wish you'd never been born. It can inflict great emotional pain. And it can, and does, reduce aspiring comedians to poverty.

Humor in speeches—like parachuting, sex in moving vehicles, and money found on the sidewalk—is best approached with cautious enthusiasm.

Don't Drop the Bomb on Takeoff

If you *must* start your speech with a piece of humor, be absolutely sure it will work. The beginning of a speech is no place to prove yourself a boorish oaf, insensitive lout, or bush league vaudevillian.

The Use and Abuse of Ridicule

Many pieces of humor get laughs by making fun of other people. Comedians openly degrade hecklers, saying things like, "When your I.Q. rises to 38, sell" and, "It's a policy of mine never to match wits with an unarmed man." Pundits and politicians ridicule other pundits and politicians, as Texas quipster Jim Hightower did when he said of President George Bush, "He was born on third base and decided to hit a triple."

Ridicule can be all in jest. But often it is not, as when Bette Davis said of a passing starlet, "There goes the good time had by all." But even when ridicule is meant in fun, it's ea´y for an audience to take it the wrong way. President Jimmy Carter was giving a speech in California when he referred to its youthful and unconventional governor by saying "Jerry Brown is California's way of celebrating the International Year of the Child." The gag wasn't particularly funny to begin with, but moreover, it reinforced the public's perception that Carter was a judgmental moralist. Carter once spoke at a banquet thrown in his honor by the president of Mexico. To the astonishment of all, he cracked a joke about being hit with Montezuma's revenge—an American euphemism for diarrhea that most Mexicans consider a racial insult.

President Carter's gaffes were puzzling to most people— the private Carter was, and is, a man of great caring and humility. And as a president, Carter was more concerned with the well-being of the peoples of other nations than most modern presidents.

The most deadly form of ridicule occurs when a speaker mocks someone who can't fight back. This kind of thing violates our ethical standard of fair play in public discourse. I'll never forget the local businessman who began his "roast" of a retiring friend by saying, "I was going to have John Belushi write my jokes for me, but he took a powder." Belushi had died just days earlier from an overdose of cocaine and heroin.

Ideally, we mark the line of decency before crossing it in ignorance.

Self-Deprecating Humor

The flip side of ridicule is self-deprecation. Here, the laughs come at your own expense. Some of the best and best-known pieces of humorous self-deprecation came from President John F. Kennedy. Under criticism that his wealthy father was bankrolling his Senate campaign, Kennedy joked at a banquet that he'd received a telegram from "my generous daddy," which read, "Dear Jack, Don't buy a single vote more than is necessary. I'll be damned if I'm going to pay for a landslide."[61]

People in high places commonly make fun of themselves to show they're not stuffy, but can recognize and accept their human failings. President Reagan practically turned self-deprecation into a national pastime. Reagan joked about his age, his acting career, his lapses in memory—anything to show that he was just a simple, sod-kicking patriot who has to turn his TelePrompTer on in the morning just like everybody else. Reagan's influence on the country was so strong that ordinary people were soon dashing from podium to podium trying to belittle themselves into greatness.

Self-deprecating humor can be effective, but it's not for everyone. The late Golda Meir put this well when she advised an associate, "Don't be humble; you're not that great."

Time and Place Matter

If you've ever fished, you know you can stand there for hours, throwing everything you've got into the water and nothing happens—then, pow, fish start biting like crazy. Likewise, audiences will nibble hesitantly on humor at certain hours of the day and lunge for it at others. Bob Orben, gag writer and chief of President Ford's speech-writing team, was one of the first to note that laughter is regulated by the emotional cycle of the business day. In the morning we tend to focus on our work, in a serious mood. At midday we've had a few hours to get something accomplished, and we're open to a few controlled chuckles. By late afternoon, the daily grind has pulverized us. We relent. We let up and laugh easily. In a way, after-dinner speeches are humorous not because they should be, but because they *can* be. Most people in America end their workweek on Thursday, Friday, and Saturday nights. So it's no coincidence that this is when people are most open to merriment in speech making.

Audience Psychology and Taste

People will laugh at things when alone or in small groups that they'll never laugh at in public. Sexist and racist jokes, ethnic slurs, scatological humor, sex jokes, "sick" humor, and the like can and often do get big laughs in the bar, on the golf course, and in other casual settings where people are with their "own kind." But tell such a joke in a public forum, or to the wrong person, and your reputation can suffer significant, possibly irreparable damage. In the space of just a few years, two U.S. cabinet members were forced to resign their posts for telling tasteless jokes—Earl Butz, former Secretary of Agriculture under President Carter, and James Watt, Secretary of the Interior under President Reagan.

A few years back, the director of the graduate psychology program at Antioch University and a few associates wrote down fifty pieces of humor and asked 241 people to rate the funniness of each on a scale of 1 to 5. The jokes were from ten categories: Nonsense, Hostile, Philosophical, Sexual, Sick, Ethnic, Social Satire, Demeaning to Males, Demeaning to Females, and Scatological (bathroom humor). None of the jokes that rated highly—ribald sexual humor and sick jabs at the less fortunate—can be tastefully repeated to a mass audience.[62]

What people commonly find funny in private will make them want to crawl under their seats in public. Even if they do *want* to laugh at it, they won't, fearing that someone else will think them insensitive, tasteless, or juvenile.

This raises another point about the group psychology of laughter: It is much easier to get people laughing if they are sitting or standing close together than if they have room to spread out. This is something to remember in planning a speech to entertain—better to select a room that's too small than one that's too big. The more space people feel around them, the harder it is to make them laugh. This is why very few comedians will consent to working outdoors.

KINDS OF HUMOR THAT WORK WELL IN SPEECHES

The Zinger

Jimmy Carter and Teddy Kennedy were vying for the Democratic party's nomination for president. At one point, Carter said of Kennedy, "I'll whip his ass." Kennedy shot back, "I knew he was behind me, but I didn't know how close."

The One-Liner

A playful piece of wit thrown to lighten the mood.

I hope you're all Republicans.

—PRESIDENT RONALD REAGAN, *to doctors upon admittance to Bethesda Naval Hospital for treatment of a gunshot wound, March 30, 1981.*

Suitable Self-Deprecation

I must say that following Arnold Hiatt on the subject of corporate day care is a little like following David on the subject of sling shots.

—LEONARD SILVERMAN, *vice president, Hoffman-Laroche, Inc., speaking on corporate childcare to the National Governors Association Conference on Day Care, April 9, 1985.* [63]

Embellished Story

When I see some of the material produced about those who toil on behalf of the cause of national defense . . . and I then observe the satisfaction which these same people nonetheless derive from the opportunity to serve, I cannot help but be reminded of a small notice I observed last fall nailed to a post at a ranch in Wyoming. It went something like this: "Lost dog. Left ear missing; broken right leg; tip of tail gone; recently castrated. Answers to the name of 'Lucky.' "

> —NORMAN R. AUGUSTINE, *vice chairman, Martin Marietta Corporation, to the National Security Industrial Association, Washington, D.C., March 17, 1988.* [64]

Witticism to Enliven the Material

Libraries are replete with books of witticisms by the famous and infamous. Injected at the right point in a speech, they can provide a rush of endorphins in the audience *and* the speaker.

He that lieth down with dogs shall rise up with fleas.

> —BEN FRANKLIN.

Being in politics is like being a football coach. You have to be smart enough to understand the game and dumb enough to think it's important.

> —SENATOR EUGENE MCCARTHY, *1976.*

Few things are harder to put up with than the annoyance of a good example.

> —MARK TWAIN.

When you begin to feel the heat, you begin to see the light.

> —SENATOR EVERETT DIRKSEN.

When we first got into office we were surprised to find out that things were just as bad as we'd been saying they were.

> —PRESIDENT JOHN KENNEDY.

Opening Anecdote to Set the Theme of the Speech

> Good morning: Some years after World War II, Winston Churchill was speaking to a group of people seated in a room about as large as this. The person who introduced him made a good-natured reference to Churchill's fondness for alcoholic beverages. "If all the spirits Sir Winston has consumed were poured into this room," he said, "they'd reach up to here," and he drew an imaginary line in the air at the six- or seven-foot level.
>
> When Winston reached the podium, he looked at the imaginary line and glanced up at the ceiling, sighed and said, "Ah—so much to be done and so little time to do it."
>
> Back in 1982, I was experiencing those same pangs.
>
> —FRANK G. WELLS, *president, Walt Disney Company, speaking on travel and tourism to the annual convention of the Travel Industry Association, Nevada, October 29, 1987.* [65]

This story had every chance of getting *at least* a few chuckles. The travel business is familiar with the consumption of alcohol in all stages. The story also lends itself to physical accompaniment—giving Wells the opportunity to expel nervous energy with his large arm and hand gestures. But note that the story would offend any Mothers Against Drunk Drivers audience, as well as most MADD members of an otherwise homogeneous audience.

Hyperbolic Poke to Belittle an Opposing View

A zinger with an aggressive tone:

> We support the visible "wonders" of health care but ignore the invisible prevention that could save far more lives. It's as if the

March of Dimes threw all its resources into iron lungs instead of helping Jonas Salk develop polio vaccine.

>—GOVERNOR RICHARD D. LAMM, *speaking to the American Hospital Association, Chicago, February 11, 1985.* [66]

Lamm's piece of hyperbole probably got a knowing harrumph from those already on his side. When savants say that humor is essentially aggressive, they're thinking of the hyperbolic zinger, the quick poke.

Despite our advanced educational system, science and technology pose somewhat of a mystery to many Americans. And it is always easier to fear the unknown and unfamiliar. . . . Consider a comparison between a nuclear power plant and a swimming pool. Can you imagine a TV camera zooming in on a pool with a grim voice-over telling us "there is enough water in this pool to drown ten thousand people"?

>—ELIZABETH M. WHELAN, *executive director, American Council of Science and Health, to the New York Academy of Sciences, New York, Sept. 22, 1987.* [67]

Funny Story to Move Things Along

There was a short account in Seattle's Zoo newspaper a while back that I think you'll find interesting:

"Circus Dwarf Franz Dasch bounced off a trampoline into the mouth of a hippopotamus that instinctively tossed back its head and swallowed him whole. The three-foot-seven-inch dwarf made the fatal mistake before 7,000 spectators in Austria who thought the tragedy was part of his act. Jane Bleyen, trapeze artist and close friend, was the first to realize that something had gone awry. She said, 'Franz was always full of surprises, but I had a gut feeling that wasn't one of them.' "

You don't have to be part of the health-care circus to know something is wrong under the big top.

>—IRMA GOERTZEN, *administrator, University Hospital, in a keynote address to the Governor's Conference on Nursing, Albuquerque, November 10, 1988.*

SIX RULES OF LIP

Humor may well be "the poetry of ideas that do not
match," "the eloquence of indifference," or "a kind of
heightened truth—super truth" (Leonard Feeney, William
Hazlitt, and E. B. White, respectively). But to work in a
speech, humorous applicants should pass a few other tests.

1. *It should be performable.* Gags that involve audience
response—knock-knock jokes, question-answer jokes
("Where does a 500-pound gorilla sleep?")—are structur-
ally inappropriate to most speeches. Consider also any potential for humorous body language and general mugging.

2. *It should be in good taste.* Screen every piece of humor
against what you know about your audience. Then ask a few
people if they think it's appropriate. If you're an important
person, your audience is always wider than you think.

3. *It should be new, surprising, fresh.* No reheated, stock
laugh-getters. Since the joke circuit is so fast, you're safer
with humor from your own experience or humor you've
created.

4. *It should serve the purpose of your speech.* Contrived
humor—"There were three men in a bar: a pallbearer, a
pimp, and a priest . . ."—is a waste of time. A listener may
forgive one such bar joke, but after that, forget it.

5. *It should be brief.* The speaker with only five, ten, or
twenty minutes to say something important doesn't have
time for a three-minute shaggy-dog story to prove a plati-
tude.

6. *It should not loudly proclaim, "See how clever I am."* Puns
and plays on words often prompt embarrassed laughter and
groans. I've never known any speaker hailed for an ability
to incite infectious groaning. Still, this is an audience call.

What to some is pompous pap is to others drop-dead funny stuff.

TRICKS AND TECHNIQUES

The Rule of Three, Again

In our look at rhetorical technique we noticed how descriptions and phrases like travelling in threes. The technique of tricolon serves humor as well. The first two set up the premise, the third drives it home.

> Critics are like eunuchs in a harem: They know how it's done, they've seen it done every day, but they're unable to do it themselves.
>
> —BRENDAN BEHAN, *playwright.*

> The best audience is intelligent, well-educated, and a little drunk.
>
> —VICE PRESIDENT ALBEN W. BARKLEY.

> The race is not always to the swift, nor the battle to the strong, but that's the way to bet.
>
> —DAMON RUNYON.

> Some men are born mediocre, some men achieve mediocrity, and some men have mediocrity thrust upon them.
>
> —JOSEPH HELLER.

> Abstract art is a product of the untalented, sold by the unprincipled, to the utterly bewildered.
>
> —AL CAPP.

The rule of three also produces good results in comedy routines. Here, laughter is built with sequences of gags on a similar theme. The first sets the direction and pulls some laughter. The second reinforces the theme. The best gag is saved for last.

> Show biz, what a racket, what you go through. I look back and shudder to think of all the women I had to sleep with to get to where I am.
>
> As a kid, I never got girls, you know? One girl called up and said come on over, there's no one home. I went over, there was no one home.
>
> One girl, in bed, she started crying. I said, "I guess you'll hate yourself in the morning, huh?" She said, "No, I hate myself right now."
>
> —RODNEY DANGERFIELD, *Seattle, March 6, 1984.*

The Shift in Premise

Much humor pops the cork of laughter by shaking and then letting go. We're riding along in one direction when the humorist jumps the tracks.

> The brain is a wonderful organ; it starts the moment you get up in the morning and does not stop until you get to the office.
>
> —ROBERT FROST.

> I have a simple philosophy of life. Fill what's empty. Empty what's full. Scratch where it itches.
>
> —ALICE ROOSEVELT LONGWORTH.

> I'm not afraid to die. I just don't want to be there when it happens.
>
> —WOODY ALLEN.

Moral indignation is in most cases 2 percent moral, 48 percent indignation, and 50 percent envy.

—VITTORIO DE SICA, *film director.*

Outrageous Statement

Psychologist Ernst Beyer, it is claimed by his students, would often attempt to shake a client off a nutty idea by going along with it for a while, then saying something completely out of character. One example had to do with a depressed patient who kept returning, session after session, to talk about how he was going to kill himself. Beyer was getting nowhere. Feeling he had nothing to lose and everything to gain, he let the client go on in the usual way for a while, then leaned closer and said, "If you're really going to kill yourself, can I have your watch?"

Look out for yourself—or they'll pee on your grave.

—LOUIS B. MAYER, *film magnate.*

If you think nobody cares if you're alive, try missing a couple of car payments.

—EARL WILSON.

How can anyone govern a nation that has two hundred and forty-six kinds of cheese?

—CHARLES DE GAULLE.

Transforming Written Humor into Spoken Humor

Humorous stories appearing in newspapers and other publications usually need some editing for smooth delivery.

First, parenthetical comments should be removed to smooth the flow of information. Next, dialogue identifiers like *he replied, she asked,* and *he inquired* should all be replaced with a simple *he said* or *she said.* Your voice will do the job of indicating whether a question was being asked or a statement is being made. Finally, words should be moved to unclutter the punch line.

Here's the *Wall Street Journal* account from September 17, 1986, of a story Ronald Reagan told Mikhail Gorbachev:

> Two men, a Russian and an American, are discussing how their nations differ. "I can walk into the Oval Office, slam my fist down on Reagan's desk and tell him I don't like the way he's running the country," the American says. The Russian thinks for a moment and replies, "But I can do the same thing in the Soviet Union. I can walk into the Politburo, slam my fist down on Gorbachev's desk and say, 'I don't like the way Reagan is running the United States.' "

In "speech-talk" the story flows better like this:

> There are two men. One's an American and the other's Russian. The American says to the Russian, "I can walk into the Oval Office, slam my fist down on Reagan's desk and tell him I don't like the way he's running the country." The Russian thinks about it and says, "So what? I can do the same thing in the Soviet Union. I too can walk into the Politburo, slam my fist down on Gorbachev's desk and say, 'I don't like the way Reagan is running the United States.' "

If you read the two versions to yourself, you're not likely to notice much difference. But if you hear them spoken, you will. Try saying them out loud.

Have a Cover Line Ready

Cover lines are critical with long stories that may flop. The
longer listeners wait for the punch line, the more disap-
pointed they'll be if it doesn't come. When a gag fails, you
want to fill the silence, separate yourself from the failure,
and move on quickly. This is the function of what comedians call a cover line. All it is is a preplanned comment ready
for use if the bit bombs. Cover lines don't have to be funny,
all they do is validate the audience's reaction and get you
out: "Well, you can't win 'em all, but that was a shutout"
or "My dog liked that joke, but he's got no taste" or "My
brother writes all my jokes. Someday I'm going up into the
attic and loosen his straightjacket," the last one used by Bob
Hope.

ONWARD

Few of us seek out speaking opportunities; they usually
arrive uninvited. Some come as beggars, willing to take
anything; some as kings, demanding the best we have.
However regal or shabby the invitation, our sense of self-
worth usually commands us to respond with dignity, purpose, and a sense of style.

This book was written to help you achieve these high
standards. It has been an ambitious book, I won't deny it.
Public speaking is an ambitious activity. As many chapters
have shown—Speech Construction, The Elements of Persuasion, and Humor in particular—speech making can be a
very complex proposition.

But I hope this book has also shown that good speech
making can be a very straightforward proposition, a matter
of following a few important rules and trying one's best to
communicate. Few speeches need to trumpet down the halls
of history. Most will succeed nicely with a more modest
objective.

If this book proves anything, it is that there's a method
to effective speech making, that it can be learned, and that

nearly anyone can do it. All of us are born speech makers. Yes, some must work harder at it than others and some, by fact of job or position, have more opportunities to practice. But happily, big improvements come early for the beginner. The heat of the spotlight is no match for the comforting breeze of applause.

Unfortunately, the enjoyment of speech making can be smothered by catastrophic thinking and obsessive concern over presentation. My advice is to study the techniques and absorb them as best you can. Then forget them and give the speech. You'll do fine. In fact, most people return from the podium exhilarated, feeling like they've been let out of a box. All it takes is the courage to lift the lid and step out.

Notes

1. *The World's Great Speeches.* New York: Dover Publications, Inc., 1973, p. 432.
2. *The World's Great Speeches,* p. 753.
3. Steven Joel Trachtenberg, "Five Ways in Which Thinking Is Dangerous," *Vital Speeches of the Day.* Mt. Pleasant, S.C.: City News Publishing Co., August 15, 1986.
4. A. W. Clausen, "Priority Issues for 1984." *Vital Speeches of the Day,* March 15, 1984.
5. Bob Keeshan, "Small Children Need Big Friends." *Vital Speeches of the Day,* July 1, 1988.
6. Richard F. Schubert, "Africa, Famine, and Compassion Fatigue." *Vital Speeches of the Day,* June 1, 1988.
7. Ron J. Anderson, "Health Care and the Patient." *Vital Speeches of the Day,* August 1, 1986.
8. *The World's Great Speeches,* p. 228.
9. *The World's Great Speeches,* pp. 729–730.
10. *The World's Great Speeches,* p. 693.
11. Garry Trudeau, "The Impertinent Questions." *Vital Speeches of the Day,* August 1, 1986.

12. Arthur Woodstone, *Nixon's Head*. New York: St. Martin's Press, 1972, p. 186.

13. Rand Araskog, "A New Era of Inventions." *Vital Speeches of the Day*, November 15, 1981.

14. Gene Perret, "Humor Is Serious Business." *Vital Speeches of the Day*, August 15, 1985.

15. Norman R. Augustine, "The Armed Forces, Civil Defense, and the Defense Industry." *Vital Speeches of the Day*, June 1, 1988.

16. Sharon Anthony Bower, *Painless Public Speaking*. New York: Prentice-Hall, Inc., 1981, pp. 17–30.

17. Immanuel Kant, *The Critique of Pure Reason*. New York: St. Martin's Press, 1965.

18. Alan H. Monroe, Bruce E. Gronbeck, Douglas Ehninger, *Principles of Speech Communication*. Glenville, Illinois: Scott, Foresman and Co., 1980.

19. *The World's Great Speeches*, p. 599.

20. Natasha Josefowitz, "I Have Arrived," *Is This Where I Was Going?* New York: Warner Books, 1983, p. 3.

21. President Ronald Reagan, "State of the Union." *Vital Speeches of the Day*, March 1, 1986.

22. T. Boone Pickens, Jr., "Restructuring America." *Vital Speeches of the Day*, September 1, 1988.

23. Robert W. Galvin, "The Power of Transformation." *Vital Speeches of the Day*, August 15, 1987.

24. Edwin Newman, *Edwin Newman on Language*. New York: Warner Books, 1980.

25. Jerry Tarver, *Professional Speech Writing*. Richmond, Virginia: The Effective Speechwriting Institute, 1982.

26. Lee A. Iacocca, "In Order To." *Vital Speeches of the Day*, October 1, 1987.

27. Alan C. Nelson, "The Sanctuary Movement." *Vital Speeches of the Day*, May 1, 1986.

28. Theodore H. White, The Bunn Lecture, Seattle, May 1984.

29. William Strunk, Jr., and E. B. White, *The Elements of Style*. New York: The Macmillan Co., 1959, pp. 15–16.

30. Dale Carnegie, *How To Win Friends and Influence People.* New York: Pocket Books, 1961, p. 95.

31. A. H. Maslow, *Motivation and Personality.* New York: Harper & Row, 1954.

32. Hans Selye, "The Stress Concept Today," in Irwin L. Kutash, Louis B. Schlesinger, and Associates, *Handbook on Stress and Anxiety.* San Francisco: Jossey-Bass Publishers, 1980.

33. Dorothy Sarnoff, *Make the Most of Your Best.* New York: Holt, Rinehart and Winston, 1981, p. 77.

34. Albert Mehrabian, *Silent Messages.* Belmont, Cal.: Wadsworth, 1971, p. 43.

35. Nick Jordan, "The Face of Feeling." *Psychology Today* 20, vol. 1, January 1986.

36. Philip Zimbardo and Ebbe B. Ebbeson, in collaboration with Christina Maslach, *Influencing Attitudes and Changing Behavior.* Reading, Mass.: Addison-Wesley Publishing Co., 1969.

37. Lewis J. Paper, *John F. Kennedy, The Promise and the Performance.* New York: Da Capo, 1975.

38. Mario Cuomo, "Your One Life Can Make a Difference." *Vital Speeches of the Day,* July 15, 1985.

39. Georgie Anne Geyer, "Is Your Generation Doomed to Live in a Second Class America?" *Vital Speeches of the Day,* August 1, 1988.

40. *The World's Great Speeches,* pp. 825–826.

41. George Bush, "Acceptance Speech, Republican National Convention, 1988." *Vital Speeches of the Day,* October 15, 1988.

42. Ann Richards, "Keynote Address, Democratic National Convention, 1988." *Vital Speeches of the Day,* August 15, 1988.

43. *The World's Great Speeches,* p. 637.

44. *The World's Great Speeches,* p. 740.

45. *The World's Great Speeches,* p. 315.

46. Daniel Webster, *Putnam's Ready Speechmaker.* New York: G. P. Putnam, 1922, p. 199.

47. Frank G. Wells, "Travel and Tourism." *Vital Speeches of the Day,* January 1, 1988.

48. President Ronald Reagan, "Life and the Preservation of Freedom." *Vital Speeches of the Day,* November 15, 1985.

49. Faye Wattleton, as reported in *The Seattle Post-Intelligencer,* October 22, 1988.

50. The Rev. Jesse Jackson, as quoted by Paul Greenberg of the Los Angeles Times Syndicate, appearing in *The Seattle Post-Intelligencer,* May 26, 1988, p. A11.

51. Anthony Mulac and A. Robert Sherman, *Speech Monographs,* vol. 42, 1975.

52. J. A. C. Brown, *Techniques of Persuasion.* New York: Penguin Books, 1963, p. 309.

53. Frank Shrontz, as reported in *The Seattle Post-Intelligencer,* June 21, 1985, p. 1.

54. E. Berscheid and E. Walster, "Attitude Change," in J. Mills (ed.), *Experimental Social Psychology,* New York: Macmillan, 1969.

55. Alan D. Baddeley, *The Psychology of Memory.* New York: Basic Books, Inc., 1976.

56. Daniel Kahneman and Amos Tversky, *Discover,* June 1985, p. 30.

57. Leon Festinger, *A Theory of Cognitive Dissonance.* Stanford, Cal.: Stanford University Press, 1957.

58. Ray Kroc, as quoted by William F. Jackson, "Goals and Adversity." *Vital Speeches of the Day,* September 15, 1985.

59. Seattle *Times,* October 18, 1984.

60. Gunderson and Hopper, "Relationships between Speech Delivery and Speech Effectiveness." *Communications Monographs,* vol. 43, 1976.

61. Annual Gridiron Club dinner, New York, 1958.

62. Harvey Mindess, et al., *The Antioch Humor Test.* New York: Avon, 1985, p. 36.

63. Leonard Silverman, "Corporate Childcare." *Vital Speeches of the Day,* June 1, 1985.

64. Norman R. Augustine, "The Armed Forces, Civil Defense, and the Defense Industry." *Vital Speeches of the Day,* June 1, 1988.

65. Frank G. Wells, "Travel and Tourism." *Vital Speeches of the Day,* January 1, 1988.
66. Richard D. Lamm, "Anti-Social Ethics." *Vital Speeches of the Day,* March 15, 1985.
67. Elizabeth M. Whelan, "Health Hoax and a Health Scare." *Vital Speeches of the Day,* November 1, 1987.

INDEX